Creative Conflict
in Religious Education
and Church Administration

Creative Conflict in Religious Education and Church Administration

DONALD E. BOSSART

Religious Education Press
Birmingham, Alabama

Library of Congress Cataloging in Publication Data

Bossart, Donald E
  Creative conflict in religious education and church administration.

  Includes bibliographical references and index.
  1. Church controversies.   2. Conflict (Psychology)
I. Title.
BV652.9.B67   254   80-12704
ISBN 0-89135-048-9

Religious Education Press, Inc.
1531 Wellington Road
Birmingham, Alabama 35209
10 9 8 7 6 5 4 3 2

*Religious Education Press publishes books and educational materials
exclusively in religious education and in areas closely related to religious education. It is committed to enhancing and professionalizing
religious education through the publication of significant scholarly
and popular works.*

PUBLISHER TO THE PROFESSION

To

MY MOTHER, MABEL,

WHO HAS BELIEVED IN ME

AND

TO

MY WIFE, GAY,

WHO HAS CALLED ME TO MY BEST

Contents

PART III
CREATIVE CONFLICT AT THE POINT OF ACTION:
SPECIFIC PROCEDURES

Acknowledgments

I wish to acknowledge those who have helped make this work possible:

Dr. James Michael Lee, publisher of Religious Education Press, who initially invited and encouraged me to write this book.

The Iliff School of Theology, which gave me a study leave in order to do the research and writing.

The Breckenridge United Methodist Church, for asking me to come to their parsonage as a study retreat for writing while being their interim pastor.

Dr. Richard C. Williams, of the Behavioral Research Institute in Boulder, Colorado, for reviewing the chapter on sociological dynamics.

Dr. Jeffrey S. Haber, of the University of Colorado at Denver, for reviewing the chapter on psychological dynamics.

Dr. Harvey H. Potthoff, of the Iliff School of Theology, for reviewing the chapter on theological dynamics.

Dr. Clarence H. Snelling, Jr., of the Iliff School of Theology, for reviewing the chapters on educational theory.

My colleagues at Iliff who have encouraged me.

Mrs. Norma Grigs, my secretary, for her patient, unstinting work typing the manuscript.

x   ACKNOWLEDGMENTS

Mrs. Gay Bossart, my wife, for her critical editing and late night typing to complete the manuscript.

And my children Kent, Alan, and Dona Gay, who have supported my efforts and borne the resulting inconveniences of family life.

Preface

The Christian church and the world around it are being rushed through a time of accelerated change, leaving people feeling a great need for security, peace, and stability. The church has always had an intent to provide sanctuary for the needy of mind, body, and spirit. People still seek out the church today, looking for answers to the deep questions of life. Those who come share a great diversity of experiences, background, values, and goals, both secular and religious. The central search for all, however, is for meaning.

Dealing with change and the correspondent learning about ourselves can be shared in a caring community, such that each of us learns from, and is supported by, the others in our diversity and our commonality. If we can learn that each has been given separate gifts and discover ways to cultivate those gifts and share them with one another, we will find that we are contributing our part to the whole Body of Christ in this ever changing world. The process for accomplishing this task may be anything but peaceful, and it may create sufficient fear and defensiveness within the participants to block the ideal results. The potential for, or the experience of, conflict may create withdrawal from or repression of the conflict rather than utilization of conflict for growth.

How will we in the church handle this potential for conflict? How this question is addressed or avoided may deter-

1

mine whether it leads to growth or destruction. The following situations are real and typify some of the regular occurrences which wait for an answer—growth or destruction.

A mother comes regularly to worship with her two young children, ages six and nine. They are very active and disrupt the service with their noise. The grandmother accompanies them and contributes to the ruckus by trying to silence the noisemakers. Many of the worshippers are older members who are unable to concentrate because of the activity. The grandmother is a pillar of the community with a strong personality. The older members of the church become so concerned that they are about to boycott the services until something is done. The pastor feels that young families should be encouraged to attend worship as a unit. What can be done in this situation for creative growth in the congregation?

A pastor comes to a new parish looking to build a strong Christian community. A faction of the congregation belongs to a charismatic group that is community-wide. This group invites the pastor to their meeting soon after his arrival in town and asks him to lead them in study. The pastor does a very good job and finds acceptance with the group. His congregation fears ruin with the charismatics' involvement with the pastor and challenges the pastor's relationship with them. How can the Christian community find unity?

A choir director starts an extensive personal campaign to replace the old church organ. She wins a number of supporters, but not a clear majority of votes to pass the official body. When the issue comes before the Administrative Board, the minister argues against the purchase. He had not been consulted by the choir director as a part of her campaign. The majority of members of the Board react negatively to the proposal of the choir director and rally around the arguments of the minister. More than several members of the Board leave the meeting feeling most irate. There is now a definite conflict between the minister and the choir director. What will happen to this staff and congregation as they try to move in a growth direction?

The Worship Commission of a church desires to attract new young members by providing two services on Sunday morning, one a traditional experience and the other a contemporary service. The traditional service is set for 10:00 A.M. and the contemporary one is set for 11:00 A.M. This is a change in time for the traditional service, which had been at 11:00 A.M. Many of the older members complain about the new hour for their traditional service being too early for them to go to church. There is really no need for a contemporary service anyway, they say. Their complaint is backed by action: they cut off attendance and financial giving. The new persons who do attend the contemporary service feel it is a great experience. What can be done in order that this community grow in the Spirit?

These real situations are examples of what goes on in almost every church community. Most of the time the conflict is a very negative experience for all concerned. It need not be! It is tragic when we lose the creative possibilities as we face opposition to our efforts in the church. It is quite easy to pick up the support given by others and turn that into new life and growth and accomplishment. What about the challenges? A vital truth is shared by W. B. Blakemore in his book of sermons, *Encountering God.*

It is the tragedy of our lives that we often mistake strong challenges for the enemy when it is our brother. Thinking it is our enemy we start to fight. If we recognize our brother, we would strive not against him but with him in a mutual search for that which is right. When we pass from enmity to brotherhood, conflict is abolished, but competition remains. . . . In brotherhood, contest does not disappear; it becomes zestful and keen as its life renewing possibilities replace its potential for destruction. (p. 28, "My Enemy . . . and My Brother.")

A basic ambivalence exists in us all when we face the dynamics of conflict in our daily lives. We intellectually affirm the good that can come from constructive conflict if we face it openly, willingly, and creatively. Yet we emotionally turn from it in fear and disdain. When we deny, suppress, or react negatively to the conflict, we reinforce our negative image of it and our association with it. Our fearful reaction is justified, setting up a future response of denial and suppression. We create a self-fulfilling prophecy.

It is my thesis that individual, group, and institutional growth in the church depends on our rational, emotional, and creative utilization of conflict that we face together in community. The conflict will be there. The question is, how will we choose to handle it?

For a creative solution, we must rid ourselves of the myth that conflict is demonic in the church. One of the ways we avoid conflict is to retreat into a private religion in order to keep the devil away. Diversity of opinion and experience, however, is not the work of the devil trying to overthrow the church, but rather the work of God's creation pumping new life into what might otherwise be a dead body waiting for resurrection. The loving person is not always the tranquil, stable, and serene person. Love may in fact demand conflict to be true love.

We face a danger in the Christian community with our increasing desire for personal, private religious experience as a means of avoiding potentially conflicting experience with our brothers and sisters in the faith. We show lack of concern for outreach, and denial of assistance from the potential support of community members. Faith is not just a love affair between a person and his/her God in isolation from others. Acceptance of others calls for the acceptance of their differences, which could mean growth for all or destruction.

The Christian community has the latent power necessary for it to avoid the dangerous tendencies described. It remains for pastors and laypersons alike to conquer their fears and respond to the creative possibilities that are provided by the diversity in God's creation. The church has grown into a strong and complex organization through this very diversity. Different expressions of discipleship exist so that all persons in the church may find a meaningful place. There are many parts to a whole, and all the parts are needed. In the process, each part calls the other to responsibility and to wholeness, for they cannot be without each other. The conflict calls us to new life. Without it, we cease being the living branches of the vine of Christ.

It is hopeful and worthy to theorize on the power of diversity and the beauty of wholeness, but not so easy to live out these ideals or see them in reality. Further education and skills are essential to help the church realize this potential. It is my hope that this book will assist in the process of bringing wholeness to the church through the utilization of conflict.

PART I

THE BASIC PRINCIPLES

1 What Is Conflict?

This chapter introduces the definitions and theory which are necessary to understand the dynamics of conflict. A good background in the sociological, psychological, and theological dynamics of this subject helps to utilize this force for growth in the church. Considerable effort flows, therefore, into grounding the reader in the theoretical aspects that are available for this understanding. Part I covers this task.

DEFINITIONS AND INTERPRETATIONS OF CONFLICT

A helpful way of understanding conflict has been given by Blaine F. Hartford of the Niagara Institute of Behavioral Science. He says that a problem is not *the* problem, but the real problem is the state of the individuals and the resulting relationship between persons. This reflects a concern for the relationship from both within and without. The inner conflict of the individual is at the base, however. According to Hartford, how one feels about one's self-worth is the keystone for understanding and dealing with all external conflict. This universal concern for self-worth is a foundation for our understanding of changes in structures, staff relationships, and group and organizational effectiveness in the church. I believe it is even at the core of our individual faith. This may seem hard to understand now, but I hope it will make more sense as we proceed in the development of conflict theory.

Conflict takes three forms:

1. Intrapersonal—I want to change, but then I'm satisfied with the way I am; the shoulds vs. the wants; self-actualization vs. status quo.
2. Interpersonal—the projection of our intrapersonal ambivalence of values onto others with the resultant dissatisfaction and frustration.
3. Intergroup—the working out of the preceding dynamics in the midst of loose or formal group structures; groups or systems relating to other groups or systems.

Conflict, in any of the three forms above, is either negatively managed or positively utilized. Conflict management usually describes the way individuals or groups react in a protective or defensive-aggressive manner. It makes use of a win/lose style in which one party must win and the other(s) must lose. Examples of this management are: withdrawal, denial, projection, polarization, coercion, or elimination. This management is usually not very beneficial for anyone concerned.

The term "utilization" reflects an effectiveness in the handling of the conflict that takes all the force and power of the interaction and turns it into the growth and benefit of all involved. Utilization requires a trusting, open, learning stance and not a defensive-aggressive one. It allows for creative movement in growth for all concerned.

A simple definition of conflict could be helpful at this point. Funk and Wagnalls define conflict as "A struggle to resist, contest of opposing forces, to come into collision."[1] This opposition of forces must be seen in a context. That context is one of interdependence. If there were not some mutual dependence between parties in conflict, consequences of such collision would not be of mutual concern to cause a problem. There must be a mutual, vital concern that affects the well-being of both parties to bring the forces into conflict. This same interdependence also offers the hope for constructive growth, since there are common values in every interdependent system. If these values are kept before the parties, then growth for all could result from the conflict, as all are pulled together by their common shared values.

One type of conflict comes from *similarities* in needs and values of the various segments of a system where the objects of need are scarce or unavailable for all. Power arises as that commodity needed to help our acquisition of those scarce objects and thus a sense of self-worth. If our needs are not satisfied, or we do not sense equilibrium in our system, we tend to fall into conflict, or competition, for the power needed for our sense of well-being. This reflects the definition "to come into collision." Two objects cannot occupy the same space at the same time, a physics lesson we often tend to forget. Because of our need for self-worth and equilibrium, we form barriers against each other's satisfaction of desired goals or needs.

This understanding of conflict does not necessarily equate with hostility or anger. Such attitudes must be acted out into "collision" behavior with another for conflict to exist, as over against merely being predispositions toward conflict. Hostility or anger may be a part of intrapersonal conflict, but until projected onto another, they do not become open, interpersonal, or intergroup conflict. They are latent. These emotions are usually kept latent for fear that they cannot be controlled, or if expressed they will be repelled by the object of the anger at the same or higher intensity level, leading to estrangement and alienation, or destruction and violence. Conflict is sharpest where bonds are strong and encompass the whole of the person. This is keenly evident in the church with its standard of commitment to a life's belief system.

Another type of conflict comes from our *differences* of needs and values amidst the segments of our systems. The different movements and motivations within the individual or group can compete for favor, with that competition for supremacy of need or value having the task of maintaining our sense of self-worth, either within or without. Unless we appreciate the contribution of differing values and ideas, our sights may fall on the winning of the battle for *our* value or idea as over against another's for our very survival and worth.* A loss of the distinctiveness of *my* idea may mean the loss of my worth. That is truly a survival situation for some.

In order to deal constructively with the above type conflict, all parties must be able to accept the uniqueness or individuality of the other as a positive gain for both parties or the whole system. This affirmation is within the concept of the Christian community and needs to be understood in order for the community to gain from conflict within it. This involves theology and both the cognitive and the affective levels of learning. More will be said later on this point.

A definition and typology of conflict have been contributed by Morton Deutsch, who has contributed heavily to this field of study. He gives a definition of conflict as that instance whenever incompatible activities occur (intrapersonal, intragroup, intranational). Or these incompatible activities may occur between two or more persons, groups, or nations.

---

*This is the tragedy of *equating* the value, opinion, issue, or outcome with the self. If my idea/value is negated, I am negated. I rise or fall as I win or lose. I do not have worth as a given; my worth must constantly be reestablished or reaffirmed.

Deutsch further tries to clarify the definition of conflict by distinguishing between competition and conflict, terms used interchangeably by some. Competition produces conflict, but not all conflict reflects competition. Competition is a win/lose dynamic. Conflict can occur where there is no perceived or actual incompatibility of goals. It can occur in a cooperative or competitive context, and resolution can be strongly influenced by the context.[2]

A typology of conflict gives further definition for us. The following six types by Deutsch are not meant to be mutually exclusive:

1. Veridical conflict—this is objective and is perceived accurately.
2. Contingent conflict—this is dependent on readily rearranged circumstances but is not recognized by the conflicting parties.
3. Displaced conflict—this is a manifest and underlying conflict which is not dealt with in the argumentation.
4. Misattributed conflict—this is between the wrong parties and, as a consequence, is usually over the wrong issues.
5. Latent conflict—this is a conflict that should be occurring and is not. It is repressed or displaced. It needs consciousness raising to be dealt with.
6. False conflict—this occurs when there is no objective base for the conflict. It implies misperception or misunderstanding.[3]

Kenneth Boulding has done significant theoretical work on the definition of conflict. He focuses on the individual as a behavior unit and uses what he calls the unit approach. Each person has behavior space, which has a position at any one moment of time. These moments are like a frame in a movie reel, and their composite forms our individual history. We get into competition as individuals when potential positions are mutually incompatible.[4]

Conflict may then be defined as a situation of competition in which the parties are aware of the incompatibility of potential future positions and in which each party wishes to occupy a position that is incompatible with the wishes of another.[5]

Boulding agrees with Blaine Hartford that the source for conflict is the intrapersonal dynamic. Boulding places the center for this conflict in the self-image of the individual. It is the mental structure, or view of the self, which sets one in the universe. This image grows as it receives messages from the outside world through the senses as well as through messages generated internally by the organism itself (the imagination).

An interpersonal source of conflict is linguistic. Our language creates symbolic images, and these images become of enormous importance in understanding human conflict because so many conflicts are over symbols. These symbols we create have great power because of the store of experiences behind them. The same symbols, however, may evoke very different meanings in the minds of two different individuals or groups, depending on what their life experiences have been. Some of the strength of our symbols comes from the ambivalence we hold toward the object. This is especially true in the area of religious experience. Those symbols toward which we hold both love and hate hold our attention. We cannot escape them because we love them. We cannot attain them because we hate them. The degree to which we are attracted by this mutual love and hate is the measure of the strength of the symbol.[6]

Our unconscious plays an important role in dealing with our images. We can have both overt and covert images. If we give exclusive attention to the overt symbols, we may be misled or surprised. Where attitudes are covert, those who are affected by them may not be able to deal with them because they are not aware of their presence. This makes resolution most difficult, often requiring the use of a third party (referee) to draw out the covert symbol meanings.[7]

In Boulding's unit approach, there is a mid-ground between the unit of person and that of formal organization. That is the group. It is a sub-population of the larger population with which the person may be identified. Groups may be formal, or loose and informal. Religious conflict is often group con- — flict rather than organizational conflict. Groups within churches may well maintain an undercurrent of conflict through their social discrimination and individual religious prejudice. These groups often interpenetrate in physical or social space, creating interpersonal and intergroup conflict. The ambivalence within the individual can often cause am- bivalence within a group, increased by the interpenetration of groups in the church.[8]

The organizational unit is the other end of the spectrum from the individual unit in this schema. The actual growth of a group into a formal organization can cause conflict where there was none before. Roles are in process of definition, and images are formed in people's minds for those role defi- nitions. Conflict then develops within and between organiza- tions.[9]

For a conflict to exist between organizations, the following conditions must be fulfilled:

1. Each of the organizations must be present in the image of the responsible decision-makers of the other.
2. A decision on the part of either executive must affect the

state of both organizations in value significant directions.

3. A decision on the part of either executive must affect the
image of the state of the other in a direction that is
regarded as unfavored.[10]

An acute problem in the perpetuation of an organization is
maintaining internal cohesion. If the roles within reward the
individuals, the organization will be stable internally. If the
roles do not reward, then the organization will not be stable
internally. Internal rewards and stability can be enhanced by
putting the organization into external conflict. For instance,
cohesion may be the result of the threat felt when a denomination decides to close a small, struggling church.[11]

Organizational conflict may also arise from new leadership
in top roles. An example would be a new pastor who is quite
different in style and personality from the past leader of the
church. The appointment of the new pastor may produce
anxieties over changing values and priorities.

Conflict may also exist between the individual member and
the group or organization. Conflict arises when the role that is
imposed on the individual by membership in the group or
organization differs from the role that the individual prefers or
thinks he/she is able to perform. A reaction can follow, such
as:

1. Acceptance—leading to either apathy or role acceptance with some meaning and adaption
2. Role changing reaction—seeking either redefinition of
role or resignation of position
3. Hostile or aggressive reaction—being expressed as
nonperformance[12]

In all cases of conflict, Boulding identifies the field of conflict as "that set of relevant variables within which conflict movements may occur that make one party worse off and one better off in their own estimation."[13]

CONFLICT AS A SOCIOLOGICAL FORCE

Conflict, as a sociological force, plays a positive role in two related yet distinct phenomena for Coser and Simmel. The first shows conflict as that force which establishes clear boundaries between groups within a social system. It does so by strengthening *group consciousness and distinctive awareness,* allowing for an identity for groups within the society. The second phenomena is that reciprocal antagonisms maintain a total social system by creating a balance between the various groups. Boundaries are kept between subgroups and their position maintained in the social system. Such a force as conflict establishes an identity and maintains *equilibrium* between groups.[14]

Sociologically understood, conflict may form around one or another of the following issues, according to Deutsch:

1. Control over resources
2. Preferences—nuisances which can merge into a struggle for power
3. Values—what "should be"
4. Beliefs about what reality is
5. Nature of relationships between parties, such as over-dominance or togetherness[15]

Conflict is a neutral reality for Deutsch. The question then becomes how to prevent conflict from being destructive, not how to eliminate it. How can a cooperative relationship evolve which will allow creative, constructive activity to dominate the interaction? This situation is described as one in which the goals of the participants are so linked that anyone can attain his/her goal if, and only if, the others with whom there is linkage can attain their goal.[16] These linkages are vital in our social organisms, helping the socialization process.

One of the seminal writers on social conflict, George Simmel, portrays his central thesis on conflict as a form of socialization. This thesis unfolds about the idea that no group or society will be entirely harmonious. Social groups need disharmony and dissociation in order to work out boundaries and identity, as well as the harmony and association to bind them together. One process does not necessarily tear down and the other build up, but both are necessary ingredients for building social relations and structure. A certain degree of conflict is therefore an ally in the formation and satisfactory continuation of group life.[17]

Another author in the early development of this thesis of conflict as a form of socialization was Robert Park. He was a part of the Chicago School that utilized conflict as a fundamental concept for social development. For Park, conflict served as the *mechanism for the achievement of self-consciousness* of the individual and for society. He saw it as constitutive for any society, bringing about an integration and a superordination and subordination of the conflict groups.

This theory of Park and of Simmel, refined by Coser, is not the only social interpretation of the place of conflict. Various contributions will be examined in the chapter on sociological dynamics. The position of conflict as a constructive form of socialization is an important thesis for this book. Suffice it to say, the field of sociology has contributed greatly to the understanding and use of conflict as a positive force in society. It should be of real service to us in the church.

CONFLICT AS A PSYCHOLOGICAL FORCE

Genetic psychology and psychoanalysis have contributed theory and evidence which point to conflict as a very important force for the establishment of ego identity and personal autonomy. This ego identity and personal autonomy give a person a fully differentiated personality from others in the world around them, contributing to a personal sense of self-worth and esteem.

Conflict also has the capacity to cause considerable anxiety, which may lead either to neuroticism or to a strong, differentiated ego. The risk is worth the taking for the satisfaction of a stronger ego and personality. This anxiety also has the potential to contribute to the strength of one's religious faith. This concept has both biblical and psychological backing which will be developed later in the chapters on psychological dynamics and theological dynamics. Briefly, the profound conflict between conscious and unconscious wills and the human and divine wills is the source of this critical anxiety and faith relationship.

Kurt Lewin defines conflict in his terms as "opposition of approximately equally strong field forces."[18] This reflects his field theory of personality which makes heavy use of the conflict of environmental forces.

An integrated psychological definition of conflict has been given by Richard Dearing in a doctoral dissertation at The Iliff School of Theology.

> Conflict, whether heavy or light, conscious or unconscious, exists where incompatible impulses seek to function simultaneously, call ego-identity into question, and through the anxiety they create, stir the ego to self-defense.[19]

Richard Dearing's research is a model for the integration of psychology and theology using the dynamics of conflict. His work will also be referred to in later chapters. This relationship of psychology and theology has much to offer the church pastor, educational director, and church lay leadership for the positive integration of conflict in the overall educational program of the church.

Ego-identity is the focus in this psychological arena relating to conflict. A pair of psychologists who utilize this terminology are John Dollard and Neal Miller. They write about two types of conflict: approach-avoidance and approach-approach. The approach-avoidance type is most helpful as it describes the intent toward an impulse-gratifying goal which is blocked by the avoidance of that same goal. The person vacillates, not being able to decide, and is disturbed by the indecision. The ego is in conflict because of the non-integrated impulses; the conflict calls the ego-identity into question.[20] This results in the state of ambivalence, which is critical to the understanding of the dynamic of intrapersonal conflict, and from that point, to the understanding of interpersonal and intergroup conflict. This particular dynamic affects that influential factor in understanding conflict referred to earlier, that of our sense of self-worth or self-esteem.

The psychological dimension of conflict just outlined gives us clearer indication of the value of conflict toward the goal of human growth and fulfillment. This human growth ties in with an educational goal of the church. Conflict has the potential to stimulate growth, the key being how it is handled. The proposal to us in the church is: conflict is inevitable and necessary if we desire innovation, creativity, and challenge as persons desiring growth and fulfillment. This means that we must choose to handle the inevitable conflict in a way leading to growth and not destruction. The mere openness or willingness to deal with conflict gives the hope that the internal dissonance will force an acceptable and positive resolution. With this push toward fulfillment or actualization, we reach out to others, recognizing our interdependence. We begin to care about ourselves and others in need of the same growth. If we can recognize our mutual needs and values as well as our own uniqueness and acknowledge the same in others, conflict can move us toward mutual growth and fulfillment.

CONFLICT AS A FORM OF INDIVIDUAL AND ORGANIZATIONAL CREATIVITY

Some view conflict as opposition, which they then respond to by resisting or fighting it, or avoiding and denying it. Both individuals and organizations tend to respond this way in order to keep the comfort of the status quo and/or the equilibrium of their relationships. We tend to prefer what we know and have experienced, as opposed to what we cannot see or know at the time. When we do this, we sacrifice the growth and creativity that lead to life-giving possibilities. To accept conflict is a risk, but worth it if we consciously try to learn skills to utilize it and allow for creativity in the resolution as individuals and organizations.

Learning the roots and dynamics of conflict and skills necessary to utilize it could be the seed for creativity and innovation rather than separation and destruction as a result of our differences. With such learning as our intent, we could bring a radical change toward a creative and committed problem-solving community in the church. Without such risk taking, we tend toward conformity which reduces the expression of our differences and permits a comfortable regularity, order, and predictability. Conformity brings a valued sense of identification and belonging. Risking the expression of our differences may stir up disorder and the anxiety from fear of destruction of our equilibrium in organizational life or interpersonal relationships. This anxiety can cause the conformity to become an end in itself and a sure road to the demise of individual and organizational creativity. The challenge to outmoded precedent is lost. What a risk! Our differences are part of the God given creation and when allowed to work for us can serve us, not destroy us. Outmoded structures in organizations can be challenged and improved through conflict utilization, leading to better ways of relating or producing toward common objectives and goals.

A concept called the "integrative approach" can help any organization toward this end. The Christian community has similar values and goals that this approach uses and seems particularly able to benefit by it. A description follows:

1. It is purposeful to goals in common.
2. It is characterized by openness.
3. Our own needs must be understood and represented accurately to others.
4. We act predictably yet flexibly without surprise.
5. There is no threat or bluff.
6. We exhibit searching behavior leading to solutions with logic and innovation.
7. We drop stereotypes and relate to ideas on their own merit.
8. What is good for us is shared with others—no win/lose.[21]

If we take this integrative approach, especially with good group processing, we are most likely to find conflict centering on issues and not personalities. This process utilizes the uniqueness and individuality of each person with a new trust and stability of relationship, leading to creative growth and fulfillment for all.

Some simple ways to foster creative conditions have been outlined by Thomas Scheidel and Laura Crowell. The conditions are as follows:

1. A continuing openness to speculation, which is to have courage to hear half-formed ideas with seemingly no strength now
2. A wide open stance to search that holds back restrictions (however real they might be) to departure from present practices
3. An encouragement of ideas from everyone
4. Genuine expression of appreciation of differences of ideas, views, and interpretations
5. A careful holding back of evaluation of any kind during the idea stage

Once such conditions are experienced, problem-solving processes can work through their various phases.

Scheidel and Crowell suggest the separation of the process into two phases. First, the diverging phase combines the elements of creative thinking: describing, analyzing, and proposing plans for management. The second phase is called the converging phase, which includes the evaluative thinking process or decision making. At the conclusion of the diverging phase, members are exercising creative thinking which leaves them with conflict and possible hostility. This storming emerges into the converging phase where the tendency is to settle into a pattern of relationships and interactions with the other members and the leader toward the establishment of norms for the organization or group.

As the diverging phase is characterized by creativity, the

converging phase is characterized by judgment or decision making and management of conflict. The latter phase moves the organization toward thinking together as a team in contrast to the separateness of the creative phase earlier. The organization is thereby kept alert, motivated, challenged to judicious thinking. It risks the facing of conflict in order that the positive value of conflict may be tapped.[23] This potential for creative growth needs to be utilized by the church. The Scheidel-Crowell proposal is shared to give an example of a plan allowing for the creativity of conflict for individuals and organizations such as the church. The preceding material lends credence to the claim by many that there is need for more inclusive theories of conflict and strategies of conflict resolution. Sociological, psychological, and theological factors need to be studied together if we expect adequate growth-releasing strategies of resolution to be developed for the church and other growth organizations. The challenge now is to make the effort to understand the sources and dynamics of conflict in order to be able to realize the creative opportunities that are ahead for individuals and organizations such as the church.

Notes

1. Funk and Wagnalls, *Standard Dictionary,* vol. 1 (New York: Funk and Wagnalls, 1964), p. 274.

2. Morton Deutsch, *The Resolution of Conflict* (New Haven: Yale University Press, 1973), pp. 10–11.

3. Ibid., pp. 12–14.

4. Kenneth E. Boulding, *Conflict and Defense* (New York: Harper and Row, 1962), pp. 3–4.

5. Ibid., p. 5.

6. Ibid., pp. 96–100.

7. Ibid., p. 104.

8. Ibid., pp. 105–107.

9. Ibid., p. 145.

10. Ibid., pp. 151–152.

11. Ibid., p. 160.

12. Ibid., p. 179.

13. Ibid., p. 153.

14. Lewis Coser, *The Functions of Social Conflict* (New York: Free Press, 1956), p. 34.

15. Deutsch, *The Resolution of Conflict,* pp. 15–17.

16. Ibid., p. 20.

17. Coser, *The Functions of Social Conflict,* p. 31.

18. Kurt Lewin, *A Dynamic Theory of Personality* (New York: McGraw-Hill, 1935), p. 88.

19. Richard N. Dearing, "The Theological Significance of Psychological Conflict: A Case Study in Paul Tillich" (Th.D. diss., Iliff School of Theology, 1970), p. 83.

20. John Dollard and Neal Miller, *Personality and Psychotherapy* (New York: McGraw-Hill, 1970), p. 366.

21. B. R. Patton and Kim Giffin, "Conflict and Its Resolution," in *Small Group Communication: A Reader,* 3rd edition, ed. R. S. Cathcart and L. A. Samovar (Dubuque, Iowa: Wm. C. Brown Co., 1979), pp. 367–368.

22. Thomas M. Scheidel and Laura Crowell, *Discussing and Deciding: A Desk Book for Group Leaders and Members* (New York: Macmillan Publishing Co., 1979), p. 171.

23. Ibid., pp. 172–199.

2 The Sociological
Dynamics of Conflict

For some people, social conflict stalks the age bearing the sword of destruction. For others, it bears the visions of the age's reconstruction.[1]

This could be a summary of the way in which conflict has been viewed by many sociologists. In this chapter, we will review the early sociological movement and then look to its definitions and distinctions, its basic shape and sources, as well as its functions. Such review of sociological perspective can be of assistance to those interested in understanding conflict and the way it might be utilized in the church.

HISTORICAL DEVELOPMENT

A look at the movement of sociological interest in conflict over the years shows considerable change. Early sociologists saw conflict as a basic interaction and valued it as good. The sociologists were reformers in society. They felt the need to change structures to make them serve people rather than limit them. Social conflict performed a decidedly constructive function.

The first sociologist to consider conflict as a separate subject, without reference to other subjects, was George Simmel (1858–1918). He dealt with both internal and external conflict, causes and results, both personal and group orientation. Simmel's work became the basis for Lewis Coser's critical restatement. Simmel's approach was that conflict is constructive as it gives rise to social change. This change is integrative on behalf of progress in society. In particular, external conflict for Simmel produces internal integration, a phenomenon of note for the church. Also, a contribution by Simmel for the church to note is that when the parties expect a high degree of consonance, slight dissonance will give rise to more intense conflict than when the parties do not expect consonance. Strangeness brings us slowly to anger because of low expectations, but once conflict starts it will become more bitter the more it is a conflict of conscience.[2]

Karl Marx adds a dimension in the developmental history of sociological conflict theory. At about the same time as Simmel, Marx was writing about conflict as basically a class conflict. In his time, workers were alienated from their work because of the machines of the industrial revolution. The object of their revolt was the ruling capitalistic class. This resultant internal conflict had its source in the existent social structure and produced changes in that structure. Conflict had its source in class interests and its role in social change.

Social Darwinism developed at the turn of the century, bringing another dimension to the understanding of conflict. Social conflict here was based on external conflict, not internal. Societies are in a battle for existence in which only the fit will survive. There is a biological element in social selection, with self-preservation and propagation as the individual's interest. This idea emerges into a conquest theory of the state. Social Darwinism rather simplistically posits that there is a process similar to biological selection as societies struggle for existence. The best ideas and the best people will win out in the competition for survival.

American sociologists come onto the scene starting in the 1920s following up the concept that conflict is fundamental and constructive in the process of social organization. Structural reform is stressed over adjustment. Robert D. Park and Ernest W. Burgess from the University of Chicago picked up on the early writers of conflict and systematized it further. The positive value of conflict continues with them as they write, "Only where there is a conflict is behavior conscious and self-conscious; only here are the conditions for rational conflict."[3] Such conflict is constitutive of any organized society. The work at the University of Chicago tended toward empiricism and became a model for other centers of study on conflict. Such empirical studies tended to be too narrow for any real development in the general conceptualization of conflict.

A second influence on conflict studies in American sociology came in the post-World War II period. Talcott Parsons led in the rise of the structural-functional theory. Where earlier writers saw the need for social change, the structural-functionists projected the adjustment of individuals to given structures. Conflict was now to be minimized in order to maintain stability with individuals and institutions. The theory reflects a systems approach in which each part has one or more functions to perform, all parts being integrated into the system by a value consensus. Conflict now becomes dysfunctional, abnormal, a disease which can be endemic to a society. This new focus picks up on words like equilibrium and collaboration, discarding the earlier interest in the dynamics of conflict and their constructive possibilities. Others like George Landberg, Elton Mayo, and Kurt Lewin centered their attention also on problems of adjustment rather than the dynamics of conflict. Integrative concerns predominated.

Kurt Lewin is one that seems to have some ambivalence as to this change in sociological attitude toward conflict. He seems to have moved from the position of the need to engage in conflict in order to maintain and insure group existence to a mood which focuses on avoidance rather than the meeting of conflict, a view of conflict which shows it dysfunctional and disintegrating. This view reflects a concern for the avoidance of conflict in what developed as "group skills." Psychology has paralleled this sociological trend with the decreasing concern in the theory of conflict and replacing that analysis by a study of tensions, strains, and psychological malfunctioning. The audience of both sociology and psychology with this point of view has consisted of social workers, mental health experts, educators, administrators, and religious leaders. Critics of the equilibrium period emerged in the persons of Ralf Dahrendorf and Lewis Coser. These post-World War II critics brought back new interest in conflict theory with the view of productive and constructive conflict. Both writers see conflict as necessary for achieving their ends of society or realizing social goals. They do disagree, however, as to what constitutes the primary ends of society.

For Dahrendorf, social conflict produces change in systems. This is necessary and good. Coercion as well as consensus becomes vital to understanding conflict dynamics. These are contradictory elements to society with conflicting values that cannot be denied by the total consensus model for equilibrium. Each dynamic, coercion and consensus, is important, but the more radical element of social change from within is important to Dahrendorf. He finds good company with Marx in the realization that internal conflict comes from the present social structure and thereby produces change in the structure. Class interest is also acknowledged as pertinent to structural change as with Marx, but Dahrendorf goes beyond such internal dynamics to allow for external factors to influence social change as well. Also, class conflicts are best understood as conflict over the legitimacy of authority rather than Marx's concern over the means of production. These class interests are never resolved, but only regulated and put within the rules of a game. These rules become very important when the groups are state-nations and war is threatened. The fullness of Dahrendorf's theory is found in his thirty-nine propositions.[4]

Lewis Coser, writing in the same period as Dahrendorf, reflects similarity with Dahrendorf's theory of conflict in proposing that conflict is good for realizing social goals. Coser's disagreement is over the primary ends of society. Coser views conflict as necessary for the stability of society, which he says is the crucial end of society. Conflict is a part of social maintenance. External conflict produces internal change, but that change is important on behalf of internal integration. Sixteen propositions are enumerated from Simmel's early thoughts and critiqued in Coser's book, *The Functions of Social Conflict* (New York: Free Press, 1956). These are seminal thoughts on the sociology of conflict and will provide a basis for further work here.

Internal community conflict as a subject found expression about this time, also. This more action-based study from particular communities added the dynamic of focus upon the commonness amidst divisiveness, bringing it into dominance in the community's concerns. All interests are recognized, but the focus is centered on points found in common. As a result of the intersecting of the various interests, a new integration is required, either with or without a new organization. It is the recognition of a new common interest amongst the parties inevitably changing all. An interlocking of community memberships may be the answer for better joint recognition and new integration and increased community identification.

At about the same time as Coser's writing, an important

work was published by UNESCO (1957) entitled *The Nature of Conflict*. It was written by the International Sociological Association in collaboration with J. Bernard, T. H. Pear, R. Arm, and R. C. Angell. Jessie Bernard wrote on the sociology of conflict in this study and contributed a distinction in conflict theory that is helpful for our purposes here. Bernard sees sociology concerned with conflict as a force affecting social systems. This is distinct from the psychological dimension which focuses upon the individual. There is some overlap. The social-psychological conceptualization of conflict is primarily an individual mechanism. Group conflict then becomes merely an additive function of individual behavior. Such conflict is essentially non-rational although not necessarily non-functional. The theoretical orientation to this approach has been referred to as the "tension" theory. This is traceable to Freud with the idea that resentments and frustration pile up until they explode in aggressive behavior. At the time of the study, these frustrations are seen to stem from the social process and not from instincts. This conflict is interpersonal, stemming from the intrapersonal tensions. A change in human attitudes and motivations is necessary to reduce the tensions. Violence is a method, but is not favored. Mental health is promoted.

Bernard proposes a more purely sociological concept which reflects a relationship between or among systems, not individuals. This is a more rational based theory which may be seen in such occurrences as schisms, secession, civil war, sect formation, splinter parties, and revolutions, as well as imperialism, colonialism, and other political, economic, and social integration. Inherent in this conceptualization is a theory of cost. Conflict arises when there are incompatible or mutually exclusive goals or aims or values espoused by persons. All may be desirable but cannot be pursued simultaneously. As a result, one must win at the cost of the others.

Practical application calls for research in strategy—how do you go about the business of winning? Hatred or hostility or violence are not synonymous with this concept of conflict.[5]

These two concepts are related but not identical. Both conceptualizations are included as bases for this work as they both apply to conflict within the church and between the church and other groups or institutions.

Jessie Bernard, writing in 1957, indicates that sociology needs a sociology of involvement.[6] Particularly seen as a problem amongst nations, cooperation and competition both need to become a part of the sociology of conflict. Social structures are needed which will allow for growth which includes both these dynamics. How can separate social systems interrelate?

In 1973, the sociologist Morton Deutsch raises this question again and addresses it himself. The question, he says, is not how to prevent conflict, but rather how to make it productive or prevent it from being destructive.[7] Deutsch maintains that this is not as a zero-sum game in which one side loses what the other gains, but rather a situation of impure conflict where there is a mixture of cooperation and competition. Both cooperation and competition are major types of conflict resolution processes, never pure but only in a predominance over one another. Destructive and constructive conflict, the focus for work by Deutsch, will be discussed later in this chapter as a focal concern by the church. Deutsch does maintain that for him the key notion is the social-psychological perspective.[8]

DEFINITIONS AND DISTINCTIONS

Delmer Hilyard presents a look at research models and designs for the study of conflict. In Fred E. Jandt's book *Conflict Resolution through Communication,* he distinguishes the model for conflict as a conflict-cooperation process.[9] That is, it must accommodate or account for a progression of changes through time. The model must also accommodate a sufficient number of differences or alternatives or incompatibilities in order to fit our real world.

Hilyard cites Coser as defining conflict in a different model scheme. Coser defines conflict as "a struggle over values or claims to status, power, and scarce resources in which the aims of the conflicting parties are not only to gain the desired values, but also to neutralize, injure, or eliminate their rivals."[10] Much conflict research has come from a perspective similar to Coser's definition. This definition is consistent with the conditions of the "constant-sum game" of game theory. Game theory is based on assumptions of rational decision-making processes, assuming well defined interests of the conflicting parties, as well as the existence of alternative courses of action. Coser is assuming status, power, and scarce resources to be the goals defining conflict.

Recognition needs to be given, however, to means, or sub-goals, as a conflict situation. The prior definition of conflict emphasizes gains to the neglect of attention to costs. In game theory, the winner of a zero-sum game has no costs. The costs are restricted to the resources within the game. If conflict management is to be the goal of research efforts, communication models are going to contribute the dimensions of gain/cost changes and bring them into satisfactory account. Conflict management, then, becomes primarily control and distribution of gains and costs, such that they become relatively small and with frequent adjustments.

COMPETITION

Another distinction is that competition is not necessarily regarded as conflict. It may be a source for it, but by itself, conflict does not assume competition. We must also differentiate such things as: antagonistic interests, misunderstandings, aggressiveness, hostility, desire to oppose, social cleavages, logical irreconcilability of goals and interests, tensions, and rivalry from conflict. These dynamics may be sources of conflict or may accompany it.[11]

Mack and Snyder give us a helpful look at conflict by citing some properties of conflictful behavior and conflict relationships. These are meant to be essential but not exhaustive.

1. Conflict requires at least two parties or distinct units. It is by definition an interactional relationship.
2. Conflict arises from a scarcity of resources. It implies mutual exclusivity.
3. Conflict behaviors in the competitive mode are designed to destroy, injure, or control another party or parties, and the relationship is one in which the parties gain only at the other's expense. The key is a win/lose relationship.
4. Conflict requires interaction in which actions and counter actions are mutually opposed. Threats are also seen as actions.
5. Conflict relations always involve attempts to gain control of scarce resources and influence behavior. It is the exercise of power. Power is defined as control over decisions.
6. Conflict relations constitute a social interaction process that has important consequences. Conflict is not a breakdown of social interaction. It is a process with important functions for the social system.
7. Conflict process represents a temporary tendency to disruption in the interaction flow between parties.
8. Conflict relations do not represent a breakdown in regu-

lated conduct, but rather a shift in the governing norms and expectations.[12]

CONSENSUS

Another distinction needs to be drawn before we go further with conflict and its sociological dynamics. Consensus has become the ideological celebration of the corporate personality today. Harmony has become intrinsic to the organization of bureaucracy—that is, in its ideal. We might think for a moment about the possibility of conflict as a means of expressing genuine social needs and aspirations. Is it not possible for rebellion to be consonant with equilibrium? And correspondingly, extreme states of consensus might create social or personal disequilibrium. It need not be stated that consensus carries an implication of social equilibrium, or that conflict entails disequilibrium. A distinction should be made between types and levels of conflict; especially between conflicts over the basis of consensus and those rising within the consensual apparatus. In either case, the theory of conflict is not tied to social disorganization or to deviants from norms. It should be recognized that both consensus and conflict are phenomena which may promote or retard social cooperation or political cohesion.

It is like the ideal of the church as the loving community. Consensus then becomes a description only of the permissive, intolerant communities, and conflict, on the other hand, is stereotyped as a theory open only to problems of coercion, pressure groups, political myths, cultural clashes, and racial strife. Conflict theory covers a wider, more profound range than this.[13]

Irving Horowitz has made an important distinction in the view of sociological theory of conflict. "Only when social function is narrowly defined as social equilibrium can a sociological theory of conflict be viewed as an overt or hidden menace to the social system."[14]

Morton Deutsch makes another important distinction noted earlier. Competition and conflict are not interchangeable. They could be interchangeable as a result of incompatibility of goals in a win/lose situation. However, conflict could also come from compatible goals in a cooperative relationship, but facing different methodologies.[15]

H. Wilson Yates gives us a helpful way of looking at conflict by distinguishing it into a "basic shape." It is a helpful series of propositions. The following then, describes his shape of conflict:

1. Conflict is an inherent dimension of social process and is essentially good.
2. Conflict is related to the achievement of whatever ends are laid out for society. In effect, the actualization of such ends is dependent on conflict.
3. Not all conflict leads to given ends desired. Conflict is understood to be separable from ends in relation to which it has arisen. The nature of conflict is instrumental and subject to initiation, regulation, and solution through strategies and structures which may be created to facilitate these actions. Conflict is subject to organization and its boundaries are negotiable. Unanticipated factors may result in consequences very different from the ends directed. Regulation, therefore, becomes important.
4. Conflict can be morally evaluated as an act in and of itself, as well as a relationship to the cause in whose services it has been commissioned. Conflict is subject to moral evaluation and institutional controls.

5. Empirical ends are those of stability *and* change. Both must exist. Restructuring may be necessary.
6. The collective interest of groups or organizations involved determine whether stability or change is needed. The public interest is central. Empirical ends are subject to moral ends.
7. Stability will be supported by those who support a given. Change is supported by those who support the given and who realize change is necessary to maintain it in the future.
8. We need a morality of ends, as well as for means for evaluation.
9. Social conflict is a clash between groups which are attempting to maintain or change some structure or structures of society in light of their own collective self-interests.
10. Conflict is not a random force or unalterable historical destiny, but rather subject to rational calculation; the organization and boundaries of conflict may be negotiated. Regulation *is* needed. Further distinction is suggested between conflict and hostility. Conflict can be amicable and is not necessarily reduced to violence. This is the primary reason why regulation is necessary. There is an expression of the positive value of the expression of hostility in conflict in that it permits the maintenance of relationships under conditions of stress, preventing group dissolution from withdrawal of the hostile participants. Such expression of hostility can clear the air, eliminating the blockage of hostile feelings and allowing freer behavior in the group than with pent up hostile feelings. Such expression of hostility can be seen as a safety valve and a valued tension/release activity.[16]

UNDERLYING SOURCES

Underlying sources are those phenomena from which conflict may result. It must be noted, however, that the presence of underlying source factors does not necessarily mean that conflict will arise.

It is generally agreed that there is not just one basic source, but multiple sources for conflict. There are some basic motivating patterns of social life which could account for a variety of conflict relations. Such patterns are: scarcity of desired objects, personal states of affairs, desirable resources in nature and culture, division of labor in organized society, social differentiation. All could lead to potentially conflictful cleavages and antagonistic interests.

This leads to two general categories of sources:

1. Those centering on interactional relationships
2. Those centering on certain internal characteristics of parties or interpersonal (personality) factors (frustration/ aggression)[17]

FUNCTIONS OF CONFLICT

It should be noted that not every type of conflict is likely to be of positive benefit, just as it is true that not every type of conflict is likely to be of detriment for individuals or groups and organizations. It does seem true that internal social conflicts which concern goals, values, or interests that do not contradict the basic assumptions upon which relationships are founded tend to be positively functional for persons and social structures. Such conflicts then, tend to make possible readjustment of norms and power relations between persons and groups in accordance with the needs felt by individuals or subgroups. An important safeguard against conflict disrupting the basis of relationships is contained in the social structure itself. This particularly refers to social structures. It is described as the institutionalization and tolerance of conflict within the structure or organization. This is a basic point of concern for Lewis Coser as he analyzes the functions of social conflict.[18] Social structures do differ in the way that they allow expression of conflict. Some show more tolerance than others.

Closely knit groups, with a high frequency of interaction and high personality involvement, tend to suppress conflict. Feelings of hostility tend to accumulate and to intensify. If conflict does break out in such type of groups, it will emerge with high intensity. This is like a delayed fuse on a bomb. The conflict that emerges does not just deal with the immediate issue. It also has to deal with the accumulation of denied expression, all in this one event. Therefore, we find the closer the group, the more intense the conflict.

In other groups where individuals only participate with less than their total personality involvement, conflict will be less likely to be disruptive. Group members are moving in many directions and are not fully concentrated either in the one group or in one conflict situation. This dynamic would sum up with the proposition that the multiplicity of conflicts stands in inverse relation to the intensity.[19] It might also be said that the intensity is also related to the rigidity of the structure. What threatens group equilibrium of such rigid structure is not the conflict, but rather the rigidity itself, which permits hostility to accumulate and channel along some cleavage once conflict breaks out.

Such functions just described have more to do with internal social conflict. External conflict deals with conflicts with other groups. Groups which are engaged in continued struggle with others must claim the total personality of their members, and therefore quash internal conflict in order to mobilize all energies for the external fight. Group unity is critical and there is a tendency therefore to suppress conflicts within.

Where groups are not involved in continued struggle with others on the opposite side, they make less claim on the total personality involvement of their members, and are therefore more flexible in structure. Internal conflicts are tolerated, and may in fact have a stabilizing influence on the structure if individuals within a group are able to have various affiliations so that their total being is not involved in any single group. This varied participation in a multiplicity of conflicts can constitute a balancing mechanism within the structure.

A further function for conflict within a group is to help revitalize the existent norms, or to contribute to the bringing forth of new ones.[20] It is a mechanism of adjustment for norms to new conditions. Warning signals are not smothered by rigid systems, and the signals are therefore picked up and dealt with before the danger point. Readjustments to the balance of power within groups can be made when necessary, avoiding the buildup of vested interests and unwarranted disequilibrium in power relations.

A very simple, but important, function of conflict emerges as the setting of group boundaries by strengthening of group cohesiveness and/or separateness. Group identity is a valued gift in which conflict can result. It becomes a part of the task of clarifying objectives for a group.

The question that arises after looking at the functions of conflict is how to guide conflict into being a productive relationship, and prevent it from being destructive. There is one critical categorization that needs to be made of conflict before looking at the constructive/destructive differentiation. That categorization is the differentiation between realistic and non-realistic conflict.

REALISTIC AND NON-REALISTIC CONFLICT

This is a helpful distinction to make within the dynamics of conflict in order to better understand how to use the function of conflict creatively and positively. Coser helps to make this distinction. Realistic conflict is defined as that which arises from frustration of specific demands within a relationship and from an estimate of gains from the participants, which is directed at the presumed frustrating object. Such conflict is a means toward a specific end. Non-realistic conflict is not occasioned by the rival ends of antagonists, but rather by the need for tension release on at least one of them. This type is not issue directed and not directed toward the attainment of a specific result or end. Failure to distinguish between these two types of conflict can seriously confuse the situation for those wanting to use conflict for growth and educative purposes.

Non-realistic conflict comes from such sources as deprivations and frustration from a socializing process and later role obligations, or from a conversion of an originally realistic conflict which was not allowed expression.

Realistic conflict should not be understood as one which is accompanied by hostility and aggressiveness. Realistic conflict is possible without such accompaniment. It may be necessary to request the assistance of a mediator in order to ascertain whether realistic and/or non-realistic elements are present.[21]

In a previous section on underlying sources of conflict, it was noted by Mack and Snyder that two sources were 1) interactional and 2) interpersonal. Realistic and unrealistic conflict can be categorized with a parallel between interactional and interpersonal sources. Realistic conflicts are presumed to have their origin primarily in interactional factors, with non-realistic conflict accounted for through non-interactional or interpersonal factors.

Another parallelism in differentiating these two categories of conflict is one provided by Rensis and Jane Likert in their *New Ways of Managing Conflict*. They differentiate the two kinds of conflict as 1) substantive, which is rooted in the substance of a task, and 2) affective, which derives from the emotional aspect of interpersonal relations. The concern they are making here is that substantive conflict is handled in an interaction even where there are affective aspects to make it more difficult. Their substantive notion is parallel to Coser's realistic conflict. Their affective conflict is parallel to the non-realistic category.[22]

CONSTRUCTIVE AND DESTRUCTIVE CONFLICT

Conflict can be a positive growing experience for all concerned, yet it can also be a most destructive experience with those involved not knowing what happened to make it so. How do we distinguish between constructive and destructive conflict and guide the course of that conflict so that it is constructive?

A definition of constructive conflict is that situation in which all are satisfied with the outcome and feel that they have gained as a result. Destructive conflict is that situation in which participants feel dissatisfied with the outcome and all feel they have lost as a result. These definitions are from Morton Deutsch, reflecting his ethical value of the greatest good for the greatest number.[23]

The course of destructive conflict tends to expand the conflict or escalate it. This leads the conflict to become independent of the initiating causes and continue after those causes have become past and irrelevant. An increase can be observed in the reliance on power, threat, coercion, and deception. Competition, misperception, and pressure for social consistency all work to further the escalation of the destructive conflict. This leads to a suspicion and a hostile attitude which increases sensitivity to differences and threats, while minimizing the awareness of similarities. The pressure for self-consistency within may lead us to an unwitting involvement in and intensification of conflict as our actions have to be justified, both to ourselves and to others.[24]

Constructive conflict, or productive conflict, is based upon the idea that conflict is not inherently pathological or destructive. It does have positive possibilities. Deutsch lists for us quite a variety of possibilities such as the following: Conflict prevents stagnation; it stimulates interest and curiosity. It is a medium through which one can hear problems and arrive at creative solutions. It is at the root of personal and social change. It can be used to do personal testing and assessing of oneself. It makes one use full capacities. It helps to establish personal and group identity. It fosters internal cohesion if conflict is external. The question comes finally to deciding what the distinctive features are in the process of resolving conflict which leads to constructive outcomes. The hypothesis that Deutsch gives us is that constructive conflict resolution is similar to the process involved in creative thinking.[25] Conflict can be constructive if it is able to arouse motivation to solve the problem. It involves the acceptance of the necessity of a change in the status quo, rather than a rigid defensive adherence to previous conditions. This touches deeply into the center of constructive conflict utilization. That is the recognition that this motivation to solve the problem and the possibility of change in the status quo must be a minimal threat to the self-esteem and self-worth of the ones likely to be changed. This non-threatening environment is critical! Threat reduces that tolerance for ambiguity and the openness to new ideas. The excessive tension can lead to privatization and stereotyping of thought (closed mind). New ideas are important for resolving conflict, and they must be free to be shared and received.

In another work of Deutsch, he goes deeper into an analysis of constructive use of conflict under the rubrics of cooperative and competitive processes. He defines the cooperative situation as one in which the goals of the participants are so linked that any participant can attain his/her goal if, and only if, the others with whom he/she is linked can attain their goals. He goes on to define a competitive situation as one in which the participants are so linked together that there is a negative correlation between their goal attainments. A participant can only attain his/her goal if, and only if, the others with whom he/she is linked cannot attain their goals.[26]

A quotation from Deutsch sums up this cooperative process for constructive conflict:

A cooperative process, by permitting more substitute ability, encourages more division of labor and roles specialization; this permits more economic use of personnel and resources, which, in turn, leads to greater task productivity. The development of more favorable attitudes toward one another in the cooperative situation fosters more mutual trust and openness of communication as well as provides a more stable basis for continuing cooperation despite the waxing and waning of particular goals. It also encourages a perception of similarity of attitudes. Since participants in the cooperative situation are more easily influenced than those in competitive situations, the former are more attentive to one another. This lessens communication difficulties and encourages the use of persuasion rather than coercion when there are differences of viewpoint.[27]

With this emphasis upon cooperation, let it not be understood that competition is all destructive. Even defeat can be constructive. It can help an individual or group have a realistic view of their power, break their illusions, and regather either individual or group in a better form than before. Loss in a competitive fashion may also help the parties see the benefits of cooperative processes over competitive ones.

What factors, then, give rise to cooperative conflict or competitive conflict? Some of the research Deutsch has done will prove helpful to us at this point.

1. Conflict instigated by fears or aversions in the conflicting parties is more difficult to resolve cooperatively than conflict instigated by desire.
2. The less intense the conflict, the easier to resolve cooperatively.
3. Conflict that threatens self-esteem is more difficult to resolve cooperatively than if not threatening self-esteem.
4. If the conflict is over large issues of principle, it is less likely to be resolved cooperatively than if it is over specific issues.
5. Conflict between parties who mutually perceive themselves to be equal in power and legitimacy is more difficult to resolve cooperatively than conflict in which there is a mutual recognition of differential power and legitimacy.
6. Unconscious conflict is more difficult to resolve than that which is recognized.

7. Conflict that is resolved by a more powerful tendency suppressing or repressing a weaker one, without the extinction of the weaker tendency's underlying motives, leads to the return of the repressed tendency in disguised form whenever the vigilance or defense of the more powerful tendency is lowered.

8. As the costs of engaging in a course of action during conflict increase, there are two opposing effects: the degree of commitment to the conflict increases, and the degree of opposition to it also increases. When the present and anticipated future costs are small in relation to the stake involved in the conflict, the readiness to increase one's commitment by incurring additional costs will increase at a faster rate than the degree of opposition; as the present and anticipated costs become equal to or surpass the stake in the conflict, the degree of opposition will increase at a faster rate than the degree of commitment.

9. There are pathogenic processes inherent in competitive conflict—such as perceptual distortion, self-deception, unwitting involvement—that tend to magnify and perpetuate conflict.[28]

Cooperative problem solving is the name for constructive conflict, it seems. It is important to cite the reasons why a cooperative process leads to productive conflict resolution. Such a list follows:

1. Cooperative problem solving aids open, honest communication of relevant information between participants. It goes beneath the manifest to the underlying issues and helps define problems. It gives more in-

tellectual resources by open flow and it reduces the likelihood of miscommunication.

2. It encourages the recognition of legitimacy of each other's interests and the necessity to search for solutions responsive to each side. It minimizes the need for defensiveness. Influence is limited to the process of persuasion rather than coercion. Enhancement of mutual resources and mutual power become objectives.

3. It leads to a trusting, friendly attitude which increases sensitivity to similarities and common interests, and minimizes differences.[29]

There is a pathology with the use of this cooperative process which is liable to be found with use in the church. It is the pathology of premature agreement. This means a superficial convergence of beliefs and values before the underlying differences can come out. This is a possibility in church groups where they are experiencing difficulty engaging in conflict and want very much to cover it over again. Some degree of controlled competitive conflict might be used to prevent such premature cooperation. Authentic cooperation is the end hoped for, in contrast to the pathology. It does presuppose an awareness that one is neither helpless nor powerless, even though one might be at a relative disadvantage. Powerlessness and an associated lack of self-esteem can work against cooperation.

Parallel dynamics to the constructive/destructive conflict divisions are those described by B. R. Patton and Kim Giffin in their study of conflict and its resolution. They refer to the two categories of distributive and integrative. The distributive situation is one which allows winning by one party only at another's expense. The integrative situation is one which allows resources to be drawn together to a common task. A further description might consider the distributive situation as a win/lose situation and the integrative situation as a win/win situation. These categories and their parallel to constructive and destructive conflict might better be seen by listing the characteristics of both approaches side by side.

DISTRIBUTIVE APPROACH

1. Purposeful behavior toward own goals
2. Secrecy
3. Understands one's own needs but disguises them
4. Unpredictable strategies, surprising
5. Threats and bluffs
6. Search behavior—both logical and irrational
7. Bad stereotyping
8. Own goals are a negation of other's achievements

INTEGRATIVE APPROACH

1. Purposeful to goals in common
2. Openness
3. Understands all needs and represents them accurately
4. Predictable yet flexible without surprise
5. No threat or bluff
6. Search behavior leads to solutions with logic and innovation
7. Ideas on own merit, positive feelings
8. Good is given for good, but can't separate from group. One loses identity to the group which is a pathological extreme[30]

It becomes important, then, to discover ways of moving either individual parties or groups from the distributive to the integrative behavior. A basic factor seems to make the major difference. The important thing is that the parties begin to know one another, and have some trust in each other. This takes the anxiety from our self-esteem and allows us to begin open communication. This idea will be developed at length under the chapter on structuring conflict for positive human functioning, as well as in the chapter on specific procedures for using creative conflict in the church.

This sociological analysis of conflict should help us begin to put together a meaningful model for the use of conflict creatively in the church. The psychological and the theological dimensions are important to complement material in this chapter as we continue to fill out a theory of conflict.

Notes

1. H. W. Yates, "A Strategy for Responding to Social Conflict," *Pastoral Psychology* 22, no. 216 (1971):31.

2. Robert C. Angell, "The Sociology of Human Conflict," in *The Nature of Human Conflict,* ed. Elton B. McNeill (Englewood Cliffs, N.J.: Prentice-Hall, 1965), p. 101.

3. Robert D. Park and Ernest W. Burgess, *Introduction to the Science of Society* (Chicago: University of Chicago Press, 1921), p. 578.

4. Ralf Dahrendorf, *Class and Class Conflict in Industrial Society* (Stanford, Calif.: Stanford University Press, 1959), pp. 237–240.

5. Jessie Bernard, "The Sociological Study of Conflict," in *The Nature of Conflict,* ed. the International Sociological Association (Paris: UNESCO, 1957), pp. 36–40.

6. Ibid., p. 113.

7. Morton Deutsch, *The Resolution of Conflict* (New Haven: Yale University Press, 1973), p. 17.

8. Ibid., pp. 7–8.

9. Delmer M. Hilyard, "Research Models and Designs for the Study of Conflict," in *Conflict Resolution through Communication,* ed. Fred E. Jandt (New York: Harper and Row, 1973), pp. 439–451.

10. Lewis Coser, "Conflict: Social Aspect," in *International Encyclopedia of the Social Sciences,* ed. David Sills (New York: Free Press, 1968), p. 232.

11. R. W. Mack and R. C. Snyder, "Conflict Theory," in *Conflict Resolution through Communication,* ed. Fred E. Jandt, p. 34.

12. Ibid., pp. 35–37.

13. Irving L. Horowitz, "Consensus, Conflict, and Cooperation," in *Conflict Resolution: Contributions of the Behavioral Sciences,* ed. Clagett G. Smith (Notre Dame: University of Notre Dame Press, 1971), pp. 66–77.

14. Ibid., p. 69.

15. Morton Deutsch, "Conflicts: Productive and Destructive," in *Conflict Resolution through Communication,* ed. Fred E. Jandt, p. 156.

16. Yates, "A Strategy for Responding to Social Conflict," pp. 32–37.

17. Mack and Snyder, "Conflict Theory," pp. 43–44.

18. Lewis Coser, *The Functions of Social Conflict* (New York: Free Press, 1956), p. 152.

19. Ibid., p. 153.

20. Ibid., p. 154.

21. Ibid., pp. 48–55.

22. Rensis and Jane Likert, *New Ways of Managing Conflict* (New York: McGraw-Hill, 1976), p. 8.

23. Deutsch, "Conflicts: Productive and Destructive," p. 158.

24. Ibid., pp. 160–166.

25. Ibid., p. 171.

26. Deutsch, *The Resolution of Conflict,* p. 20.

27. Ibid., p. 24.

28. Ibid., pp. 46–47.

29. Deutsch, "Conflicts: Productive and Destructive," p. 176.

30. B. R. Patton and Kim Giffin, "Conflict and Its Resolution," in *Small Group Communication: A Reader,* 3rd edition, ed. R. S. Cathcart and L. A. Samovar (Dubuque, Iowa: Wm. C. Brown Co., 1979), p. 368.

3 The Psychological Dynamics
of Conflict

Anxiety

There are several terms which are important to understand as we move into this psychological dimension of conflict. The first of these terms is *anxiety*. *Anxiety*, defined by Funk and Wagnalls' *Standard Dictionary* (1964), appears as a disturbance of mind regarding some uncertain event. The significant word in that definition is the word *uncertain*. The object of anxiety is usually unknown. Symptoms of anxiety and fear may be felt from conscious or unconscious conflict. Anxiety often arises from the tension caused by incompatible impulses which involve fear. The danger signal is the anxiety feelings.

Anxiety feelings with no ready explanation produce varied responses. This stems from anxiety having two components, according to a study by Schacter and Singer (1962). These two components are: 1) physiological and 2) cognitive. The physiological component shows in the physical system as increased heart rate, respiration changes, goose bumps, or some other physical form of sensitivity. This response of the body is giving a signal. The next concern, however, is to interpret that signal. This forms the second component of anxiety, the cognitive dimension. It need not be self-evident that increased heart rate results from a fear reaction. It may be a reaction of excitement and anticipation of a favorable experience. The study by Schacter and Singer indicates that the person who experiences a physiological arousal will tend to label this state in terms of the information currently available to him/her.[1] Others in the environment can interpret false value to a situation. Or a person will respond to a situation with avoidance because he/she has pre-labeled it bad or fearful. A person can overgeneralize or draw on inference not warranted by the situation, either from false labeling of his/her own or by influences from others also present. Later, a person may learn that the label of aversion to a stimulus was in error. A person may label a stimulus situation vicariously and never know the actual circumstance or validity of the labeling. This differentiation of anxiety between the physiological and the cognitive dimensions gives us some interesting possibilities to understanding how persons respond differently to conflict situations. The interpretation of a stimulated physiological condition arising from conflict can be learned from a negative, fearful model or a positive, anticipatory model. We learn our responses from the responses of others to similar situations. If we observe others experiencing fear and aversion to conflict, we are likely to respond in the same way, or vice versa. We can learn positive responses to conflict if we have positive models before us. What a challenge to pastoral and lay leadership in our church communities as they provide models to others.

Richard Dearing proposes another way of looking at anxiety in his dissertation at The Iliff School of Theology. He cites anxiety as the emotion of being between, of being in conflict, with no real object. Philosophically, anxiety is the fear of the loss of the self in accepting freedom. Freedom represents the possibility of the unknown, of lack of control of the future. The question of the self in the future engenders the anxiety. Anxiety becomes the crux of conflict when it is expressed through the struggle for the meaning of being. If we experience meaninglessness in life, we are driven to search for meaning. Anxiety reflects the struggle between the meaninglessness of life and the potential for meaning or being.[2] How very important positive modeling becomes.

Hostility

Another term important to understand in our pursuit of the psychological dynamics of conflict is the term *hostility*. The same dictionary defines *hostility* as the state of being hostile, or having a spirit of enmity (antipathy, hatred). Hostility needs to be understood as an attitude or a sentiment which may or may not emerge as conflict between parties or groups. It indicates a predisposition to conflict behavior, but may or may not culminate in it. The expression of hostility in conflict can serve a positive function when it permits the maintenance of relationships under stress, preventing group dissolution which could occur through the withdrawal of hostile participants. Where structures are rigid, which they often are in the church, differences are not allowed expression, and the disgruntled persons have no way to express their hostility or dissatisfaction. They have no recourse but to leave the organization or the church. Some have withheld financial support as their expression of hostility, but are not allowed to get into the interaction of conflict which might find resolve. A clearing of the air must come through interaction along with the expression of hostility. If that hostility is allowed to accumulate without healthy discharge, substitute objects may be selected for the original, thereby confusing the situation. If the hostility comes out in substitute objects, this may act as a safety valve function for the preservation of the organization, but it will not promote growth and development. If hostility finds no healthy relief, it can lead to disruptive outbreaks as a result of the rigid structure and the accelerated intensity of negative feelings.

Hostility is not necessarily a temporary mood of anger, but can be a way one participates in this world. This has significance in our present consideration of conflict. Hostility arises from the ambivalence felt as we participate in the basic dichotomy of life, living between love and hate. Freud sets this in terms of life and death instincts.

Aggression

This leads to the next term which needs description and interpretation. That is the term *aggression*. There are psychologists like Freud who have attributed conflict to a basic aggressive instinct in human beings. The source is a drive that we humans have that leads us either to cause destructive acts of hostility over against one another or acts which serve to be constructive to our social organization.

Freud's life force (Eros and Thanatos) is dualistic and ambivalent, being at once creative and destructive. Love and violence are quite interdependent, establishing a very basic intrapersonal conflict. These two forces need an equilibrium to maintain a healthy dialogue with life, personally and socially. When we lose a sense of this equilibrium or balance, we resort to violence as a means of overcoming our felt weakness. An axiom, which is attributed to Georges Gusdorf (*La Vertu de Force*, Paris, Presses Universitaires de France, 1957) affirms that the stronger one feels, the less one needs to show one's strength. Therefore, an equilibrium minimizes conflict, maintaining a balance between love and violence, strength and weakness.

Research done by Konrad Lorenz and reflected in his book *On Aggression* (translated by Litzke and Metheun, London, Harcourt Brace, New York, 1966) provides some basis for getting at the issue of good and bad aggression in regard to conflict dynamics.

Natural aggression need not necessarily be destructive but constructive in the task of building up the community. Aggression directs a natural process of selecting leaders to organize and rule, preventing chaos. This process shows up as a natural part of the animal kingdom. Human civilization experiences more destructive violence than the defensive, order-producing dynamic of the animals. Animals seem to have an instinctive conservation of the species as demonstrated by their restraint in not killing one of their own. Man does not always show this. It is this instinctive veto which is manifestly absent in man who is capable of annihilating his whole race.

So long as animals live in flocks or undifferentiated bands, no destructive aggression shows up among them. Only anonymous relationships exist. Among the territorial animals, there appears the personal differentiation which is the necessary condition for the development of personal feelings, attachments, friendship, and love. These are part of a more progressive social organization. Aggressiveness proves to be a necessary condition for social evolution or progress and with it the expression of love. It is a gift of life which can be used for good or bad, present in *all* of us, consciously or unconsciously. Aggressiveness, like conflict, has a potential for destructive or constructive consequences. For some, aggressiveness may be that necessary ingredient in life which proves that we exist as individuals in this mass society.

The difficulty we have with aggressiveness in our society stems not from its mere presence, but rather from our deficiency or loss of limits. Violence is hard to stop once started, growing with each experience in chain reaction and escalation. As Lorenz pointed out, animals show natural constraint. Law has become man's only restraint.

Rene Girard gives us some guidance in distinquishing between good and bad aggression involving violence. In the book *Violence and the Sacred* (Grosset, Paris, 1972), this Frenchman separates out two kinds of violence, not content to accept only a matter of degree. Girard builds on the reference of Jesus to two kinds of prophets: false and true. You will know them by their fruits. Girard develops two categories for violence:

1. Reciprocal violence, which divides people, building up to greater and greater conflict.
2. Inaugural violence, which is as a sacrifice. All can find themselves united by this act which saves the community and inaugurates a new society.

Religion is a link between these two. It can compensate for or annul the reciprocal violence by ritual violence. The destructive is rechanneled to beneficent ends. Paul Tournier gives an analogy to illustrate describing a powder barrel which is poured out just as it was about to explode. As the powder pours out, it turns into cement which is used to make firm the foundations of community.[3]

Girard suggests that festivals of nations are acceptable places to work through innate violence. Discharge comes through extravagance, orgies, physical exertion, etc. It might be said now that we are past the festival stage and have only wars to do this work for us.

Psychotherapy has given us a substitute investment for violence in its therapeutic catharsis. It does the job for us now that primitive blood sacrifice did many years ago.

Sports are probably the most active, accepted social use of violence. This activity gives us both active and passive investment for our natural aggression.

Some psychologists think that aggression is not instinctual at all, but rather based on a reaction to frustration. John Dollard and his associates have described aggression as a consequence of frustration. Dollard writes concerning this theory in his book *Frustration and Aggression* (New Haven: Yale University Press, 1939). It is the development of frustration that causes us to make aggressive acts against one another or groups against one another.

One approach to the frustration theory postulates that frustration and low tolerance put a cap on the emotions rather than a regulator leading to a buildup and eventual explosion. The explosion comes in either verbal or physical violence when the frustration level has exceeded the tolerance level of the individual or group. This does not stem from an innate instinct, but rather is a reaction to pent-up forces coming from the personal environment. One must learn how to deal with frustration in both intrapersonal and interpersonal relations.

Assertiveness training programs often approach aggressiveness as a learned skill and attitude. This training affirms that you can learn to be assertive and overcome to some degree a personal past or environment. If reflects a learned attitude and not an instinctual drive as the base. Reinforcement and social modeling all contribute to the learning process for a healthy, assertive attitude in interpersonal relations, even for aggressive behavior which may appear to be instinctual. The use of power and authority can be learned ways of response to situations which challenge us, not the expression of unconscious, innate behavior.

Another critic of the instinctual or innate explanation of aggression and conflict as well as the simple frustration theory is Anatol Rapoport. He debates the assumption of a frustration base for aggression since he finds it impossible to see aggression as a necessary or sufficient consequence of frustration. If it is frustration that is the cause, then we must expect that aggression always follows frustration even though it may occur in other situations unrelated to the frustration. The absence of overt aggressive reaction at the time of frustration doesn't mean that such reaction tendencies are not there. They may be only sublimated. Frustration may be a cause of aggression and therefore conflict, but not the sole or basic cause.[4]

As to the matter of deciding whether or not aggression is instinctual or learned, I do not wish to conclude the matter here. I merely want to show the dynamics of aggression as they relate to intrapersonal and interpersonal conflict.

Our aggressiveness may also be coupled with a defensive reaction and lead us to a certain reaction pattern in our management of conflict. Such a defensive/aggressive pattern could lead to responses such as denial, withdrawal, noncompliance, projection onto others, polarization into "them" versus "us," coercion, or just the simple win/lose pattern.

Ambivalence

The theory of aggression in relation to conflict brings us to another term called ambivalence. Rapoport maintains that the aggressive instinct could not be demonstrated by conspicuous excesses of "man's inhumanity to Man."[5] Cruelty could be matched by kindness. Rapoport goes on to indicate that all specifically human faculties are ambivalent, and all of our works are potentially both blessings and curses. This phenomenon of ambivalence can be further understood by the theory of Dollard and Miller as they delineate two conflict types. The first is the approach/approach and the second is the approach/avoidance. The second seems more likely to help explain conflict here. The approach/avoidance conflict style occurs when the approach to an impulse-gratifying goal is blocked by the avoidance of that same goal, or something intimately connected with it. The person vacillates, not being able to decide, and is disturbed by the indecision. The ego suffers conflict because a non-integrated impulse confronts it, and the effect is both to approach and to avoid the goal. It is like the situation in which one feels the need to do well, but that feeling is countered by the feeling of inferiority. Dollard and Miller add another dimension described as avoidance/ avoidance conflict. Here the subject must choose one of two undesirable alternatives. The subject vacillates between the two, feeling it impossible to integrate a chosen alternative.[6]

In another way, ambivalence may be described as that conflict between love and hate. We find it acceptable to express the love, but not acceptable to express the hate. When we try to hide the hate, however, the feelings come out in other misplaced or indirect ways. This creates inner conflict which we project out into the outer world. When we feel this inner ambivalence between love and hate and don't necessarily see it expressed by others in the outer world, we feel the need to project that conflict "out there." When we are able to do that, the world is consonant with our own personality structure within, and we feel more comfortable. If the conflict isn't already out there, we will project it. That conflict emerges out of our own personality needs from the ambivalence within.

Ambivalence might be described as a drive and counter-drive within each one of us. On the one hand we feel the need to actualize our potential, to be that which we are not yet, and at the same time feel the need for the security which the status quo gives to us. We are in constant tension between our self-actualization drive and our drive to remain as we are.

Dissonance

We do strive to maintain some consistency within ourselves. When inconsistency shows, we try to deal with it or to rationalize it away. We are not always successful in either endeavor. Leon Festinger suggests that we replace the word *inconsistency* with the word *dissonance,* and that we replace the word *consistency* with *consonance.* He then projects a basic hypothesis. The existence of dissonance in our lives, being psychologically uncomfortable, will motivate the person to try to reduce this dissonance and achieve consonance. When dissonance arises, in addition to trying to reduce it, the person will actively avoid situations and information which would likely increase the dissonance. The presence of dissonance gives rise to pressures to reduce or eliminate that dissonance. We respond to those pressures by changing our behavior or affecting the knowledge or cognitive element which has created the dissonant feeling. Sometimes, it is difficult to change our behavior. This forces us to another route—that of changing the environmental cognitive element. This holds particularly true for the social environment, but is much harder to accomplish for the physical environment. In order to eliminate a dissonance completely, some cognitive element must be changed, and that is not always possible. A last resort may be to reduce the dissonance by adding some new cognitive elements to reconcile the difference. This may result in reducing the value or importance of the dissonance.[7]

We get into this cognitive dissonance at a very early age, according to the worldview construct that Blaine F. Hartford has devised from basic transactional analysis. Blaine Hartford, director of the Niagara Institute of Behavioral Science, maintains that basic cognitive dissonance starts with birth and goes to seven years of age. He maintains we are grinding the lenses of our sight during this time (personality development). We try to take in information from the *real* world and relate it to our *my* world. Since we have imperfect lenses, some of the real world does not get through, or we decide not to accept that information, or some of it gets through distorted. What does get through comes into our *my, now* world. There must be congruence with this *my* and *now* world. By the age of seven, we have developed the separation of these two worlds. Our energies go into achieving equilibrium between these two worlds for both predictability and sanity. Without this equilibrium, we have an untenable tension. We have a need to know or control this *now* world that we allow in from the *real* world and have it controlled by our *my* world. If we need to, we will reconstruct this *now* world to get equilibrium. This is how we handle conflict. It is easier to change our *my* world, but we always try to influence the *now* world in order to maintain a status quo. This just forms another way of trying to understand the concept of cognitive dissonance and the basic dynamics of intrapersonal conflict.

The conflict theory of Virginia Satir further interprets our continuing attempts to deal with the need for congruency out of ambivalence. She sees us dealing with this need for congruency by reacting in at least four different ways. One way we handle it is to use placating or the blocking out of oneself in order to respond to another's demands. A second way of responding is to resort to blaming or the blocking out of the other person in order to allow ourselves to come to the center. The third response is the correct/reasonable one which allows for the blocking out of both self and the other person in the name of reason. The fourth pattern is the response which makes the situation irrelevant, blocking out the self and the other and the context of the conflict. All of these attempts reflect the individual's need to have congruency with both internal and external dimensions.[8] How we handle our cognitive dissonance or our need for congruence becomes a critical factor as we come to the point of our conflict management or its utilization.

The Unconscious and Conscious Will

One other factor needs to be considered as we prepare to go into further depth with our psychological understanding of conflict. We must realize that both an unconscious and a conscious will exist in each of us. Freud has given us the basic background for the understanding of both conscious and unconscious levels of the personality. Conflict can exist between what we consciously will and what we unconsciously will. This fits into the understanding of our previous terms of ambivalence and anxiety. We have difficulty getting at the unconscious will. Sometimes, we must go into dream therapy. The important point for us here, however, is to recognize unconscious needs (intrapersonal conflicts) which do motivate our behavior (interpersonal conflict). Our unconscious needs can therefore direct the life of our conscious will for their own gratification. When our unconscious needs direct our outer behavior, we can find ourselves in conflict which is very difficult to resolve. There is too much distance between the cause and the behavioral effect. Hostility can arise in this way separated from the original object of ambivalence and conflict, making it difficult to deal with the conflict. It becomes very important that the conflict be moved from the unconscious level to the conscious in order to find resolve. This presents a vital opportunity for the activity of a caring community such as the Christian community working amidst conflict. Loving acceptance can be a critical ingredient to free a person to receive the unconscious ambivalence and to accept it openly and consciously with others' assistance without a fear of rejection or loss of worth.

The above theory finds good illustration in vocational choices. A vocation must fulfill both conscious and unconscious needs. Conflict usually arises when the unconscious needs are directing the vocational choice. Unconscious, repressed needs may be the base for conflicts in the choices clergy make. Margaretta Bowers, in her book *Conflicts of the Clergy,* suggests that such elements as death or abandonment by a parent figure can often lead a person to the choice of ministry. These early, infantile dependent needs go unfulfilled and lead the person to repressed anger and aggressiveness. Fear of the unleashing of this aggressiveness creates the choice for a church vocation. The church or the congregation holds the security for the cleric meeting dependency needs through "mother church," keeping him from expressing the destructiveness in his personality. Only when these unconscious needs can be brought to consciousness can there be a more fulfilling sense of vocational choice and the resolution of the inner conflict through more conscious congruence.[9]

INTEGRATED DEFINITION OF CONFLICT

Having concluded the preceding introduction to psychological terms or dynamics for conflict, I wish to posit an integrated psychological definition of personal conflict. Richard Dearing again contributes to our study. His definition follows: "Conflict, whether heavy or light, conscious or unconscious, exists where incompatible impulses seek to function simultaneously, call ego-identity into question and through the anxiety they create stir the ego to self-defense."[10] This definition focuses on the concept of ego-identity. This identity provides a central phenomenon for our personality, warranting our particular attention to it in this study.

EGO-IDENTITY

Conflict, from a psychological point of view, moves like a continuum from the personal to the social dimension. The one affects the other. The personal will be the emphasis in this discussion.

Most of us are aware of the contribution which Sigmund Freud has made to understand personality dynamics by the use of the terms *id, ego,* and *superego.* The dynamics of the personality are created by drives and counterdrives. Conflict, by the previous definition, occurs when incompatible drives seek simultaneous expression and are or are not integrated into the personality. Where the drives or impulses cannot function simultaneously, the resulting conflict occurs in the ego. Conflict exists where ego-identity is called into question by the presence of simultaneously functioning impulses within the person. The id forms the center of the instincts which reflect biological needs or impulses which seek satisfaction. These instincts operate on a pleasure principle for instant gratification. Where the drives or impulses conflict, the ego must regulate this gratification according to a reality principle. The instincts may be repressed or gratified by the ego's regulation. If the instinct finds neither gratification nor acceptance in consciousness, a neurotic symptom may develop. The basic theory may be illustrated by the following diagram:

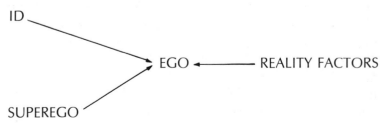

The ego forms the conflict region of the personality. The personality meets the world at this point. The ego must regulate reality factors with the personality's internal factors. The person seeks the balance between the internal state and relation to reality. When our self-image comes into conflict with reality factors impinging from the outside, we find an experience which calls our ego-identity into question. This conflict must be registered at a conscious level to be dealt with. If we keep it at the unconscious level, then it may well become a part of neurotic behavior, or at least displaced conflict. One can be overwhelmed with the ego-identity crisis when the ego cannot handle the conflict. The ego has the capacity to grasp and shape the objective reality impinging upon it. When it cannot handle this impact, the ego may go into despair. This can become a theological problem and will be discussed in the theological chapter. The ego finds integration and has a secure self-identity when all aspects of the self are united comfortably. The frequent tension felt within the ego as the internal forces of the person and the external forces of reality meet becomes the source of our conflict. This has been referred to as intrapersonal conflict. Interpersonal and intergroup conflict follow as a result of this ego tension. The individual longs for a clear and decisive ego identity. The ego becomes the crucible of our life according to Freud's theory.

A study by Dollard and Miller referred to earlier gives us another overview. Their approach/avoidance concept reflects conscious intrapersonal conflict dynamic. The approach to an impulse-gratifying goal can be blocked by the avoidance of that same goal, or something intimately connected with it. The person vacillates, not being able to decide between the approach impulse and the avoidance impulse. The indecision disturbs greatly. The ego finds itself in conflict because of the non-integrated impulses which are demanded. The effect is both to approach and to avoid the goal, calling the ego-identity into question. The inner conflict unresolved leaves the person with a low sense of self-worth and acceptance illustrated by the experience of being called into a situation where one needs to do well but is countered by the feelings of personal inferiority.[11] These feelings of inferiority or low self-worth and acceptance have significant influence in the individual's dealing with conflict. The problem of self-acceptance provides central focus for this writer in the understanding of conflict and its management and utilization.

SELF-ACCEPTANCE

The most fundamental of all human needs calls for experiences which will build and maintain the individual's sense of personal worth and importance. All persons have this strong inherent desire to achieve and maintain a sense of worth and value. We respond to experiences of life on the basis of their perceived relation to our values, goals, traditions, and expectations. This motivating force to confirm our personal worth causes individuals to seek membership in groups whose values are consistent with their own and strive to be valued by such groups. This force directs the individual to engage in behavior which will achieve the goals of the group. Each person in the group is open to the influence of the others because they are in the same group with the same values and motives for fulfillment. This results in basic cooperative behavior. The root of it all lies in the desire and need for significance, self-worth, esteem—the confirming of the inner self-image by the selected outer reality.

The state of well-being of the individual surfaces as the vital balance which affects the relationship between persons and the potential for how conflict will be handled. The battle in the ego over conflicting impulses of personal want vs. feelings of "should" or "ought" is critical for the state of well-being or worth. We desire a positive sense of mastery over the threats of the ego conflict with an acceptable ego-identity. All internal conflicts are based on the results of this inner encounter.

Sometimes our personal desires or self-image feel very uncomfortable and unacceptable, either to ourselves, or we anticipate them to be similarly received by others. We usually repress them. Looking deeply into ourselves, we don't like what we see. We resort to rationalization and self-deception in order to live. We live in the fear and the threat of our "darker side" being expressed or discovered. Our interpersonal relations become very fragile when we are in this condition. We may be excessively concerned about our own power and control over others when feeling this way. Usually a power drive by an individual has deep roots in his/her fundamental human need for self-worth, for significance, for esteem. Unfortunately, it is a distorted form of self-affirmation. More on this dynamic will be forthcoming in the chapter on power.

Theologically, this dynamic can be translated into humanity's need to be reconciled internally with the self, with the rest of humanity, with life as a whole. We begin to recognize our estrangement and alienation from our true being, or the center of being. Internal and external authority must find integration for our comfort and well-being. Support and nurture become imminent needs.

Ego-identity and self-worth are related through the dynamics of the structural elements of the personality as seen by Paul Tillich in his *Courage to Be*. He states the intrapsychic conflict dynamics to be the following:

Conflicts between unconscious drives and repressive norms, between drives trying to dominate the center of the personality,
between imaginary worlds and the experience of the real world,
between trends toward greatness and perfection and the experience of one's smallness and imperfection, between the desire to
be accepted by other people or society or the universe and the
experience of being rejected, between the will to be and the
seemingly intolerable burden of being which evokes open or
hidden desire not to be.[12]

This dynamic merges into the theological dimension to be
discussed in the chapter to follow. Resolve, or healing for this
conflict, comes through knowing we are ultimately significant
and valuable, regardless of the problems of life. Healing
comes from the experience of being counted and experiencing
that joy.

Self-acceptance is perhaps the basic criterion for mental
health, as well as for our integrity of knowing. Psychotherapy
sees it essential for our health to come to terms with the "I
wants" in our life. Repression can lead to neuroticism and a
negative self-image. I stated earlier that the intrapersonal conflict in us all takes form in the battle between the "I wants"
and the "I shoulds" within us. How we handle this basic
encounter within delineates how we shall handle the interpersonal encounters of our life. Self-acceptance describes the
coming to terms with this conflict. If we can achieve self-
acceptance, then we become open to knowing the truth
about self, others, and the world around us. It is the beginning
of self-actualization. The freedom to be and accept that being
leads to the beginning of receptivity to others and their possibility for being, uniting in a win/win situation of relationship
which delineates conflict utilization from mere management.
This condition allows for the goals of self and the goals of

others to be compatible, fostering creativity and growth for all concerned.

The core of self-acceptance for John F. Haught, in his writings on the subject, includes both the reconciling to our personal limitations as well as the awakening to our possibilities.[13] This allows the individual to accept the self when he/she cannot measure up to the idealized self and yet not accept the present state of being as final in the quest for new possibilities within. This state reflects the appreciation of knowing something and yet not being resentful for not knowing everything. We find acceptance for what we are and also expect that we will grow beyond that.

Our ability for self-deception sets us up for the need to prove our positive side above our dark side and to enter into the win/lose dynamics of conflict, needing to overcome the other with our position and goals. Our need makes us unable to recognize other positions or even be open to the possibility that our combined goals might have some mutual possibilities for fulfillment.

If we allow for growth, both for its experience in us and its further potential in us, this growth generally brings forth both a sense of self-esteem and worth and an increasing anxiety in the face of the future. This anxiety can send us back to an earlier state of existence, putting us into a defensive mood, with self-denial and closed relations tending to lead us into conflict with others. What makes psychoanalysis successful, when it is so, is the mood of acceptance that the therapist conveys in the relationship, permitting the patient to express the feelings and desires not allowed out before because of the fear of their unacceptability. This finds its parallel in the theological sphere. One can feel the acceptance of the unacceptable in either case.

Achieving self-acceptance leads to the possibilities of new

growth out of the conflicts of the present, creating the openness of mind to include others in the process and allowing for growth by all. Effective conflict utilization involves the state of the individual and the resulting relationships. The dynamics of self-acceptance prove vital to the state of the individual and are projected into relationships.

SELF-ACTUALIZATION

We experience both a drive toward self-actualization and a counter-drive to maintain the status quo within each of us. The majority drive seems to be the one for maintenance of the status quo. What about our self-actualization?

Self-actualization involves risk. The security of maintaining one's status quo entices the individual to negate the freedom and new possibilities that are a part of the self-actualization process. If we maintain that every person is original and unique, having only the task of discovering his/her uniqueness and developing it, then it becomes necessary to affirm the freedom to grow and to take the risk of the drive toward self-actualization. Each individual must affirm this freedom and possibility for growth. One cannot do this by oneself. It requires a cooperative relationship of self with others in an actualizing community. If the individual cannot affirm that freedom and take the risk, self-identity will not be actualized. There will be a basic ambiguity and feeling of fragmentation. The resulting insecurity and ambiguity become the source of our intrapersonal, interpersonal, and intergroup conflict. The fear of self-destruction in the process of self-creation leads to this chaos. Each of us has needs for internal security and the degree to which these needs are satisfied will be the degree to which the individual can risk in self-actualization.

It takes internal power (as well as external support) to

achieve self-identity with self-integrative functioning. We become integrated when all aspects of the self are united in a single identity. Self-alteration is the dynamic element of self-actualization. It designates the establishment of a new center of identity which is actual, not potential. It actualizes a new center of identity under the principle of growth. The individual is free to form new concepts of the self and to intend to actualize them.[14]

Both psychology and theology have proponents who maintain that all of us long for an unambiguous fulfillment of our essential possibilities. We desire our identity to be set clearly and decisively. For total fulfillment, the individual seeks to actualize the unity of being and meaning. Self-actualization can bring its own meaning. Fear does arise, however, that our change will be aimless and that we will find ourselves driven in all directions without definite aim or content.

One of the forms of control over this fear of aimless change and meaningless form is the relationship in community. As indicated earlier, other persons in community can become indispensable in the fulfillment of our given potential. They become catalysts and contributors. They can also form a nurturing, supporting, caring surrounding.

In the encounter with others in the community, the individual's drive to fulfill his/her potential may be blocked by the drive of others. However, from this encounter with others may spring transformations that might not otherwise have happened without the encounter in community.

The dynamics of self-actualization include the establishment of a self-identity with some comfort and security about its integration, the recognition of the potential for change toward increased self-realization, the taking of the risk of the freedom necessary for self-alteration, and the reintegration of the new experience into new self-identity and affirmation.

The conflict comes in the fear of self-disintegration if the freedom and risks are taken for self-actualization. A strong ego and a strong community of support help most in this process.

Driven by the search for self, identity, and actualization, we take on a critical need for meaning. The dimension of the movement toward meaning takes us beyond these psychological dynamics and leads to the theological.

Notes

1. S. Schacter and J. E. Singer, "Cognitive, Social and Physiological Determinants of Emotional States," *Psychological Review* 69 (1962): 379–399.

2. Richard N. Dearing, "The Theological Significance of Psychological Conflict: A Case Study in Paul Tillich" (Th. D. diss., Iliff School of Theology, 1970), pp. 4–9.

3. Paul Tournier, *The Violence Within* (New York: Harper and Row, 1977), pp. 61–64.

4. Anatol Rapoport, *Conflict in Man-Made Environment* (England, Penguin Books, 1974), pp. 126–132.

5. Ibid., p. 122.

6. John Dollard and Neal Miller, *Personality and Psychotherapy* (New York: McGraw-Hill, 1970), p. 366.

7. Leon Festinger, *A Theory of Cognitive Dissonance* (Stanford, Calif.: Stanford University Press, 1957), pp. 1–22.

8. Virginia Satir, *Peoplemaking* (Palo Alto, Calif.: Science and Behavior Books, 1972), pp. 63–95.

9. Margaretta K. Bowers, *Conflicts of the Clergy* (New York: Thomas Nelson & Sons, 1963), pp. 231–234.

10. Dearing, "The Theological Significance of Psychological Conflict: A Case Study in Paul Tillich," p. 292.

11. Ibid., p. 73.

12. Paul Tillich, *The Courage to Be* (New Haven: Yale University Press, 1952), pp. 64–65.

13. John F. Haught, *Religion and Self-Acceptance* (New York: Paulist Press, 1976), p. 62.

14. Dearing, "The Theological Significance of Psychological Conflict: A Case Study in Paul Tillich," p. 215.

4 The Theological Dynamics
of Conflict

The psychological conflicts just reviewed in the preceding chapter do have religious and theological significance. The ego was isolated as the psychic center, or that structure which negotiates life in the organization of our being. Theology deals with that meaning of being for us. Tillich defines theology saying, "Theology is the normative and systematic presentation of a concrete realization of the concept of religion."[1] The primary conflicts of life, expressed in the ego, are considered the deepest issues of life in which persons are asking questions of their identity and meaning as part of their ultimate concern. As people ask for ultimate meaning, they pose the question of God. Ultimate meaning is our goal, and conflict expresses the awareness of both the pains and the dreams of that goal.

The theological dynamics could be described in an interpretation of the first term that was studied in the psychological dynamics chapter—*anxiety*. The term *anxiety* was defined as a disturbance of mind regarding some uncertain event, with the significance around the word *uncertain*. The object of anxiety is usually unknown. With a philosophical interpretation, anxiety expresses the fear of the loss of self with the acceptance of freedom. Going further into a theological interpretation, anxiety might be seen as the crux of ontological conflict, which is that conflict in life that expresses struggle with the meaning of being and choosing to be as a creative person. God, in the Christian faith, creates life as good and meaningful. If we experience meaninglessness, we are driven in search for that meaning. Anxiety, then, is the struggle between the meaninglessness of life and the potential of meaning or of being. In the theology of Paul Tillich, this is expressed in the term *ultimate concern*.[2]

Psychological terms can have theological dimensions. How then does a theologian understand psychological conflict? Dearing offers an outline for such understanding:

1. The theologian identifies the life issue experienced in the conflict.
2. The theologian identifies the question applied in the conflict, which is humanity asking the question about itself.
3. The theologian identifies and interprets the depth dimension of the conflict. This refers particularly to the question of meaning of being.
4. The theologian recognizes that the conflicts need to be healed, not covered up.
5. The theologian relates the symbols of the faith to the conflict of existence. The problems of existence are united with the answers of theology. This is identified as Tillich's method of correlation.[3]

Not everyone expresses conflict in ultimate concern, but the theologian presents the structures which lift the conflict to the ultimate. In sum, then, the theological significance of psychological conflict is the expression of the primary conflicts of life processed through the ego, asking questions of identity and ultimate concern.

There is a twofold test of the theologian on the task assignment. The following questions arise:

1. Can the theologian recognize, expose, and clarify the conflicts of human existence in which the ultimate issues of life are raised?
2. Can the theologian express the way in which the healing power of the Gospel speaks to the conflict of existence?[4]

We can look further, then, at presuppositions for a theology of conflict.

1. Psychological conflict describes one of the crucibles of life. It occurs when the person is called into question by incompatible impulses originating either from within or without the person, or in combination.
2. The person in psychological conflict is estranged from that which would give comfort. The person longs for relief from pain.
3. Psychological conflict is raised to its ultimate dimension when it is elevated to the question: What is the person's ultimate meaning in life? This identifies two levels of conflict. One is the immediate concern; the other is a concern for meaning in life.
4. The depth conflicts of existence are healed when the meaning of the person's life breaks in upon him/her. The surface problems of life may always be present, but they may be negotiated out of the experience of meaningfulness.

5. The Christian Gospel is a concrete realization of healing in which persons learn the meaning of their lives. It speaks to human need by speaking to the depth concerns of life.

6. The experience of being healed is knowing one is ultimately significant and valuable, regardless of the problems of life. It is the discovery of being counted as one of the loved ones of God, and experiencing the joy of counting.

7. The ministry of conflict is seeing, hearing, and knowing the conflicts of existence; witnessing to the experience of being healed; making healing available to others.[5]

TWO THEOLOGICAL POSITIONS

There are two major theological positions that I wish to relate to the dynamics of conflict. There are other possible positions, but these two reflect major differences of approach.

The first theological position starts with an all-powerful, transcendent God reaching out to an alienated humanity which needs and seeks reunion with the Creator. God is a being who stands over against the world and acts upon it from a transcendent position. God has sent the message of hope to a humanity alienated from Himself through the new being of Jesus, the Christ. The healing which makes humanity whole is given once and for all through this redemptive act. It remains for each person to reach out and accept this gift of grace from above, overcoming the conflict within the self and between the self and God. The estranged person can do nothing about the basic conflict but accept the condition and the grace of the solution. Until resignation to the condition and acceptance of the grace, life appears ambiguous and absurd in its contradictions and lack of meaning. The sinful response comes in the act of trying to overcome our finitude and apparent hopeless, helpless condition and trying to be God. Hope must triumph over anxiety in order to live with meaning.

This state of alienation and need for redemption from beyond has been described as humanity's fall from unity with God, a universal disorder. The only hope is to look beyond creation to the Creator for a redemptive act. This disorder of humanity can be described as an imbalance in the polarity of life. John Macquarrie, in his *Principles of Christian Theology,* cites human existence as polar in nature, creating a most ambiguous situation for living. These polarities are described as possibility and facticity, rationality and irrationality, responsibility and impotence, anxiety and hope.[6] The tension of these polarities of life force us to seek order to the disorder, or balance to the imbalance. Life most often is experienced as disequilibrium and disorder in need of resolve. We must make sense of existence, find meaning in our inner and outer relationships, restore order to our disorder in one way or another. The need for hope beyond our anxieties may well sum it up. This hope comes from beyond us all, from the transcendent God who has redeemed us by his act of love through Jesus, the Christ. The conflict or polarity of existence, the disorder of imbalance, has found resolve. Humanity's quest for meaning has been met by God's gift of meaning through grace.

The second theological position that speaks to our conflict of existence posits a God as a "creative activity that underlies, permeates, relates, and sustains all finite realities."[7] This does not reflect a God over against the world, acting on it from outside as described earlier. This idea of God shows forth as "the dynamic personal Spirit who is the ultimate ground of all being and becoming, and who through manifold interrelationships seeks the maximum realization of value."[8] This

God, whose creative activity sustains our world, seeks to develop a community of supportive persons to work with Him and each other toward self-realization and world-realization. This work is not without frustration and temporary failure. We live in the midst of an unfinished process, continuously in conflict and imbalance or disorder, but yet in the expectation and hope for meaning and full realization of the potential of all creation. God's presence makes the difference, as both God and humanity strive for the completeness of creation or the realization of its values. God has invited us to co-author creation with Him. This co-creation toward providential ends for all creatures brings the meaning and fulfillment we seek. God is the ultimate ground of hope and meaning, providing the resources for the achievement of creation's ends.

Given a concept of a God who seeks the maximum realization of value, conflict or polarity can be accepted without severe contradiction or loss of meaning in life. If creation is yet to be completed, and we as God's creatures are called to be co-creators in the unfinished business, it isn't difficult to conceive of the value of each person as he/she contributes to the ongoing process from the perspective of their God-given uniqueness. The appreciation of the individual's unique value, so necessary for understanding this conflict management model, becomes integral to both the theology and the conflict theory. We are all called into the ongoing, long, and sometimes painful evolution of the natural order and the arduous endeavors of human history. The frustration of conflict will be very much a part of the co-creation, but the resources of our Co-Creator are more than adequate to actualize the total potential for full, eventual value realization. Meaning comes through participation in the process with hope. Conflict management and utilization makes positive use of all contributions as potentially valuable in the evolving of the creative process in problem solving. The theology of a God whose creative activity permeates our world and who seeks to form a community of mutually supportive persons to strive with Him and one another goes along well with the consensus model of win/win conflict management. Facticity and possibility can be accepted together as part of the ongoing nature of things. God becomes acceptable as one who is incomparably great, yet less than omnipotent through His very own design. Creative activity of God and man together involves costly travail as a result, making the crucifixion all the more significant to humanity. Suffering, though not ordained of God, may contribute to growth of character. This idea becomes all the more meaningful when God shares the pain and pathos.

The affirmation of positive gain out of the experience of the conflicts of life becomes easier to accept if one can see resources available to face the inevitable chaos of the process. S. Paul Schilling contributes a theology to bring meaning to suffering and anguish that often must be endured in either destructive or constructive conflict. God does provide, he says:

1. His presence gives strength and courage to endure and overcome.
2. God works through human agents to alleviate and prevent suffering.
3. God gives hope by conserving and building on the contributions we make to the ends He seeks. God and creation grow through the continuous actualization by His creatures. Our labors do not go for nothing, giving a meaning to the whole of life.
4. God keeps those who trust and serve Him by giving them life beyond physical death. This allows for the free undertaking of the risks of life.
5. Providence is active in social relations and processes of

history as well as in the lives of individuals. He seeks to
guide the actualization of values as both Judge and De-
stroyer of Evil, as well as Creator and Redeemer of the
Good.[9]

This theological position provides for the necessary assur-
ances for meaningful involvement in conflict, overcoming our
natural fears of the risks and the need for the defenses we
often raise.

The other general theological position cited earlier actually
can come to the same effect on the question of meaning in
conflict. The transcendent God, who redeems humanity from
the fall, bringing persons to Himself by His one act of grace
gives the assurance of meaning for life amidst our fears of
conflict and anxieties of death. God's redemptive act, rather
than His shared creative activity, reconciles humanity to
Himself, breaking down walls of separation between God and
persons and between person and person—or even intrapersonal separation. Persons are freed from the anxiety of life
which was described earlier by Tillich, allowing for creative
movement toward actualization of life in its fullness. Defensiveness raised against the fear and risk of conflict becomes
unnecessary, freeing the constructive process that allows for
actualization for all in a win/win style. Polarities are overcome and ambiguities lessened, freeing life from its absurdity
and lack of meaning. Balance becomes possible, reordering
the distortion of sin and alienation. Looking beyond humanity
to a grace given by God, we become grasped by that for
which we have been dimly and ignorantly seeking. The initiative comes from above and beyond with the gift of meaning
and grace. Our hope is in the revelation of a new understanding of ourselves and our relation to each other and our God. A
new union of love and life makes all things possible that

before seemed impossible, including our view of the conflicts of life which we face. The lost are found and given new life through the new relationship to God through Christ. The possibility of balance and order out of imbalance and chaos gives the hope and meaning so necessary for growth and actualization. Conflict becomes tolerable, ambiguity finds new possibilities.

Meaning must come from the process of actualizing our God-given potential, discovering what it is in community, and striving for its realization with the help of others and our God. Conflict provides the testing ground for the gathering of resources from God and one another, stimulating growth where otherwise stagnation and self-satisfaction set in. Conflict becomes intolerable where it threatens who we are or who we might become, and separation from our ultimate realization in and with our God. Hope and love become critical dimensions. Hope must be present in order to avoid the meaninglessness that can come from disorder and chaos in conflict. Love must be present to provide support in the working out of the process of conflict. God must provide for both hope and love in order to give meaning to the conflicts of life. These two theological positions cited in this section provide the possibilities of hope, love, and meaning in different ways, yet the outcome of either allows conflict to be a constructive, creative force for us all.

A MAJOR ISSUE—DEALING WITH OUR FINITUDE

How persons deal with their finitude has considerable bearing on how we deal with the conflict dynamics which are produced. With the theory that all conflict begins in the intrapersonal dynamics and then is projected out onto others and between groups, how we deal with our finitude becomes a central issue.

For some, living is a burden and there is a constant struggle in order to attain relief from the realization of one's finitude, or limitations in the living out of life. The acceptance of our finitude does project the idea of God, and our living under that power. In the New Testament, Paul projects this conflict as the conflict of the will. In the eighth chapter of Romans, the classic conflict of the divine will vs. the arbitrary will is referred to. It is that of being caught between the will of the flesh over against the will of the spirit, or the self over against God. The Old Testament reflects this conflict in Psalm 38 as the writer shows the pathos of being caught in the battle of the wills. Persons seem to be driven by this conflict within to seek out a new life of relationship to God. Some, as Augustine, wish God to solve the question of relief from the conflict; others feel the need to be reconciled with themselves, with humanity, with life as a whole. Feeling estrangement, alienation from our true being, translates into a need for reconciliation or acceptance of one's self and one's finitude.

The selfhood notion is a key one according to the theologian John Macquarrie. He maintains that existence fulfills itself in selfhood, in which the polarities of existence are held in balance. This self is not solitary, but rather finds possibility only in a community of selves, amidst the polarities of individuality and community. The self does not come ready-made but is merely a potentially for becoming. We attain selfhood then in a matter of degree of realization. The attainment comes only so far as the person looks beyond the limits of the self for the master concern that can create a stable and unified self. This includes the acceptance of the factical aspects of existence (finitude), which must be taken up into the potentially which one projects for the self into the future. The past must be accepted and a commitment made to a new future. Resources come from beyond us as finite creatures according to our faith stance. Finitude, therefore, is not a limiting concept according to Macquarrie, but rather must be accepted in order that a realistic future may be attained.[10]

Paul Tillich sees our battle with finitude as fitting into the category of sin. Sin translates into the finite trying to be infinite. The product equals despair. Tillich describes despair as:

> ... the conflict between the will to maintain one's self and the will to lose one's self; to maintain one's self by gaining the whole world, thus acknowledging through one's infinite desire the unity and totality to which one belongs, and to lose one's self by returning to the natural servitude of living below the level of freedom, thereby acknowledging that freedom is the inescapable presupposition of despair.[11]

The dynamics of conflict flow from this definition as follows: If one chooses this servile condition of living suggested above, persons become objects alongside other objects of the world. They are not subjects grounded in God's being. The person becomes object, through which the servile self-center gratifies its own need to be the ground of being. Consequently, the person is driven against others in self-destructive struggle. Existential anxiety develops, analogous to the situation of the isolated individual facing the abyss of nothingness and the threat of annihilation all around. This leads us back to the basic psychological dynamic of anxiety.

In the chapter on psychological dynamics, the ego was cited from Freud's theory as the center of the person in which the internal dynamics of wants and shoulds had to deal with the reality factors externally impinging upon the ego. This was the psychological center of the person. Tillich, in his theology, suggests that this psychological center be referred to as the spirited ego for theological interpretation.[12] This personal center is the psychological center transformed over into the dimension of spirit. Spirit is referred to as the unity of meaning and power. This spirited ego risks the creative freedom and the existential anxiety, accepting the risk of living with one's finitude, overcoming despair. Spirit, then, becomes the power to grasp one's destiny and to find and give meaning to it. Herein is the theological resolution to the internal conflict. However, it is a risk to choose to be in control of life choices and define who you are.

Persons strive for a recognition of a God as one in whom their finitude is conquered. An interdependence of the ego, self, and world develops which results in a livable ontological structure.

Dealing with our finitude not only creates anxiety, but it creates the second psychological concept which was described in our last chapter. If we see ourselves as over against God, as in the category of sin, we are in the power struggle of our arbitrary will vs. the divine will. Our battle over against God develops hatred and hostility as a result of our imposed estrangement. This estrangement is not only over against God, but over against neighbor as well. We can develop a defensive posture over against the whole world.

Gordon Jackson finds meaning with this struggle of person over against God and humanity by utilizing a theology from Karl Barth.[13] In this approach, Barth represents the biblical-theological point of view that poses hostility within the human community as a derivative from the hostility between persons and God. The theological dynamics go as follows: hostility begins by saying that there is no God. It is the culmination of the pride of humankind. Christ is rejected and haunts persons who want to orient life around themselves.

The freedom of Christ is rejected. Persons refuse to be themselves by loving God, who alone can guarantee them their selfhood. God becomes the advocate of the freedom that persons reject. God continues to love and accept persons who reject Him. Shame and guilt are further dynamics of this hatred and hostility. Persons become isolated from neighbors, but in the process of this isolation, they continue in their ontological relationship to God, carrying with them their hostility. This hostility is continually provoked by God not letting the person alone. Grace becomes the offense, for God then is in a position of daring persons to live higher than they can imagine.

This theological condition of hostility to God is translated into the hostile, defensive relationship to neighbor. The dynamic moves from intrapersonal conflict to interpersonal conflict. Theologically, this hostility participates in the disrelationship between God and persons and the alienation of person from person. Jackson describes it thus: "It is the emotional concomitant of man's defiant NO to God's affirming YES, this being the primal stage and dimension of hostility."[14] Jackson proposes that the aggressive instinct, about which Freud theorized, is this primal hostility toward God which is repressed at such a deep level that it appears as an instinct. This repressed energy would give the drive its force which is so manifest within the human community. The resultant dynamic is guilt. The problem, then, becomes how to establish our self-esteem and worth.

Gordon Jackson refers to Alfred North Whitehead's concept that how a self relates to its past constitutes what the self is. The past presents an affective tone to which the subject responds. How the self feels its world determines the constitution of the self. The result is the problem of self-worth, a concept critical to the understanding of conflict.[15]

SELF-WORTH

The result of the battle of the finite or arbitrary will vs. divine will, and the hostility that has developed through that battle, can lead to the battle within the soul that is typified by Paul's experience. Prior to his conversion, Paul thought that he knew himself very well, and that he was exercising his responsibilities with sound personal judgment. His persecution of Christians was, in his mind, a righteous act and affirmed his own personal integrity. His denial of the freedom presented by Jesus, the Christ, was finally overcome in his self-transformation, releasing the energy that was repressing this freedom and allowing for the sudden dramatic shift in the God of his life. The transition to a new sense of God, as Father of Jesus, the Christ, allowed him to confess his previous self-deception. This represented a new turn in his quest for meaning—a revised story of God as Creator and Redeemer which allowed Paul to accept himself and his past. The God of Jesus Christ was seen as the God of unconditional acceptance, acceptance irrespective of a person's attempts to achieve salvation by works. Self-deception is a mechanism that we use in order to accept what we see deep within. We, as persons, resort to rationalization and self-deception in order to live. We need a religious story which establishes a world which eliminates the fear of uncovering our darker side. It allows us this quest for truthfulness, a basic desire within us all. Paul, like Martin Luther, was continually making efforts toward self-justification and found he was unable to continue his self-deception. He could not live up to the ideals projected by the law. Both Paul and Luther had, within their own theological training, some intimation of the unconditional character of divine love. Conversions take the form of the sudden flooding of this unconditional love into the consciousness, overcoming the need for self-deception and self-righteousness. Acceptance of that new freedom is the dramatic conclusion of conversion. All of the energies of repression can be released, and the self has a new bond to life which is positive rather than negative. There is a diffusion of one's energy that fields the elements of combat and conflict within the self to allow that energy to move into self-discovery and the use of the new freedom. There is a new, dynamic, vital relationship with the world around the person—with God and with neighbor. John Haught sees this dynamic of conflict resolution, philosophically and theologically, as illustrative of how a religious narrative revision can promote the process of appropriating and coinciding with one's basic spontaneities.[16] This acceptance of the self always requires some immersion of story in which the whole self can be reshaped. Philosophy and theology point the way. Intellectual powers cannot do the job alone. What makes the whole endeavor successful is the surrounding mood of acceptance that in psychoanalysis permits the patient to express the feelings and desires which have been buried due to social unacceptability. In theology, it is God's unconditional love, felt and experienced by the person, which promotes the quest for truthfulness toward one's self—an acceptance which makes that freedom to be one's self a reality. One is accepted in any case. Nothing that can be done or left undone can change this basic acceptance. There is no longer any need to hide from one's self; the person is free in the true meaning of the term. The only barrier to that freedom is the refusal to accept the fact that one is accepted. The refusal is rooted in the will to power, the desire for mastery, the need to overcome the feelings of finitude.

John Haught sums up our situation well as he describes the need for each of us to say "yes" to ourselves because of the "yes" by God. Theologically and philosophically the image of God is creative and motivates believers to a grateful acceptance of their being, in spite of the discomfort felt when we review what we have achieved in the quests of our lives. This acceptance can free one to take part in the creative process. Without a sense of gratitude, our discomfort can become turmoil. It can be filled with the hunger for power, with resentment and indifference. With the image of God as unconditional acceptance, however, it is possible for persons to remove their self-deception and accept a God of redemptive love who says "yes" to persons on the basis of friendship rather than coercion. This dynamic frees persons to make that symbolic sincere "yes" to themselves.[17] In reflection, it looks like we have been taken full circle back to Tillich's anxiety and our basic need for reconciliation with our self, each other, and with our God.

Martin Luther's own theology and experience has the potential to contribute to our understanding of theological dimensions of conflict. His own intrapsychic conflict is illustrative of intrapersonal, psychological, and theological dynamics. In fact, Luther's experience has been made the basis for a model of creative conflict for learning in Christian education by Robert L. Conrad.

Self-acceptance and self-worth are the basic dynamics behind Luther's personal conflict and theology. His sense of self-worth was negatively influenced by one system of theology which he had called scholastic theology. This scholastic theology emphasized the ability of persons to refrain from sin and move toward God on their own free will. This first step had to be taken before God would grant grace to help reach the second step, the full saving grace of Christ.

A second theological system was at war within Luther with this first scholastic system. In his own growing theology (drawn mostly from his study of the Bible and from St. Augustine), Luther learned that persons are justified by grace, not by works. Righteousness is given only to the faithful. Such contradictions with scholastic theology put Luther into despair at times, leaving him frustrated and feeling unworthy.

Luther entered into a series of steps that are important to understand in order to view the creative use of conflict. The first step was the stage of active struggling with his two opposing points of view. This created deep intrapersonal conflict in Luther. He wanted a gracious God, but he experienced a judging one. His sin seemed to dominate. The predestination influence in scholastic theology seemed to put God into an arbitrary decision-making process.

The second step in Luther's experience was that of passive resignation. He met a problem that seemed insoluble, and he did not know where to turn. He turned to silence and meditation.

The third step is described as unexpected insight. That insight was the discovery of justification by faith. The righteousness of God comes as a gift of God to persons and not a demand upon them. People cannot work toward that righteousness. They can only receive it as a gift freely given in faith. The image for God now is a gracious one.

The final insight was that in Jesus Christ the will of God is revealed to save those who believe. The fourth step in the arduous process for Luther was the long-range theological interpretation. Integration was needed to take care of both the negative and positive aspects of person and God. God is finally defined as one who is both a gracious and judging God. God judges through the law but saves through the Gospel. Luther's theological integration took years, but provided a new kind of peace for him. The struggle continued between flesh and spirit, but his theology had a new redeeming function for him.[18] This theological conflict within the life of

Luther provides the resource for a model for education. This will be discussed in the appropriate chapter in Part II of this book.

The dynamic in Luther's four steps is a movement away from basic conflict within and its loss of self-worth and esteem and a need for a sense of value, integration, and worth.

SELF-ACTUALIZATION

Self-actualization is tantamount to what we might call growth or the pursuit of truth about oneself. Self-acceptance provides an important preliminary dynamic. Both Luther and St. Paul stand as good examples. Both men spent considerable energy in the process of self-deception in their efforts toward self-justification. They were unable to make their own spontaneous striving coincide with this effort toward self-justification. Neither man could measure up under the law. Paul suddenly felt the congruity of the followers of Jesus and desired that same integration of life that they seemed to possess. He found the expression of his deepest feelings in the Christian story and upon accepting the unconditional love of the Christian Gospel, he was finally able to find liberation from his fanatical pharisaism. Luther's own self-discovery and acceptance of unconditional love came more from his own meditation and study of the scriptures. Both Paul and Luther received new psychic energy diverted from their attempts for righteousness under the law and became open to new strivings for truth, unafraid of what they would find within themselves. It all was finally acceptable. The self-actualization process could begin with new energy, new openness, and spontaneity in the pursuit toward the truth about themselves and the world around them. A new religious story made new life possible. The only barrier now could be the refusal to accept the freedom of their acceptance. It seems that self-actualization requires some such freeing religious story.

Basically, conflict exists between who we are existentially and who we could be within our essential natures. Our ego-self is simultaneously aware of the two mutually exclusive possibilities. As we know psychologically, the ego-self is the center for the resolution of this basic conflict. Tillich maintains life is the actuality of being. This ontological philosophy unites both essence and existence—an apparent basic polarity. Everything faces the threat of falling from being into nonbeing, which is an end to actualization or death. The spirit center of life urges the person to seek meaning, transforming the psychological potential into an actual person in search of the meaning of existence.[19]

Self-actualization requires power. That power must be freed within the individual as a result of the self-acceptance found by unconditional love. This new affirmation of the spirit recalls our potential and feeds our striving to seek to actualize that potential. Persons desire a centering of life which unites the self, the neighbor, and the experience of the world.

But the self-creation of life always carries its ambiguities. If growth is going to create new centers for our identity, or transformation of our old identity, there is the danger that chaos will result, and the possibilities of self-creation will fall into self-destruction instead. There is a tension between the movement toward creation and toward destruction. We look for the balance and the affirmation that we are free to move ahead. Faith through one's religious story seems to be the key. Self-actualization, theologically speaking, is the effort to grasp and fulfill the ultimate meaning of our being. It is the actualizing of the unity of our meaning and being. The ambiguous condition of self-actualization motivates us to find the bridge of ultimate concern or that faith in our potential being.[20]

Theology deals with the meaning of being and therefore contributes to our intrapersonal conflict situation, the source of all our conflict. Theology helps us understand the power which is necessary for self-actualizations. We will be dealing with power later in a separate chapter, but it must be understood in the relationship to theology. Power needs to be understood in this context not as a dominating force, but as a force that helps persons fulfill their richest possibilities in the interactions of the human community. Power has a positive import in relation to the moral and religious grounding of our lives.

Power has its rootage in our basic need for self-esteem, or self-worth. Used for selfish ends of domination and control, it is a distorted form of self-affirmation. Reinhold Niebuhr acknowledged this struggle for the moral use of power in his book, *The Nature and Destiny of Man*. Power can be a tool to use in order to compensate for limitations as human beings. It can lead to our quest to be God, to be over all things. Both Tillich and Niebuhr saw this form of power as the basic sin of man and woman. We can get the full power of our beings realized through creative appropriation of our limits. It does require the embracing of all our life. It is possible to encounter a block with others who are in a drive to fulfill their potential. However, from encountering others may well spring transformations that would not have happened without the encounter. Other persons become indispensable in the fulfillment of our given potential. They enact the role of catalysts and contributors. The strength of the Christian community shows itself best in this manner. The expression of care and love in the mutual task of helping one another discover potential and develop it carries tremendous power. Power becomes a positive concept using its force for mutual fulfillment and not for self-domination. The need to dominate dwindles when one feels the full acceptance and unconditional love of God and neighbor. Power is not basically a scarce commodity for which we compete but rather an expandable dynamic awaiting release from within as well as from without in creative interaction with other persons. The maximum development of power consists of mobilizing the resources of all in pursuit of common, compatible goals. This power is within the grasp and the experience of each within the Christian community.

The New Testament message embodies this concept of power. It is not against power itself but rather demonic forms of power. The concept of justice forbids the use of power by an individual or group within society to impose its will on the whole of society.

Divine power has a very interesting parallel with our human power. An interpretation of the gospel discloses a God that reveals Himself as an inexhaustible reserve of power striving to realize forms of life which have been created. That power does not mean that the divine force can do whatever He pleases as a tyrant. In and through the self-actualizing of His own creatures, He creates and fulfills His own being. It is an enabling, energizing, empowering presence whose own fulfillment is inextricably bound to the fulfillment of all creation.[21] God's presence is to break through our violence to each other and to energize and bring to fulfillment life's possibilities in the human community. This is the Christian's path toward self-actualization with the help of the Christian community. God's presence provides the renewing, redemptive resources to deal with ambivalence and frustration in order to find meaning in the midst of it all.

This direction is both rationally and theologically sound. None of us as individuals is equal to God. None of us has the complete truth. Any idea or action on the part of us as finite individuals is subject to error. Instead of rejecting others' ideas, we ought to be seeking them. By so doing, we can find more accurately where our possibilities lie and find the support necessary for our achievement and betterment. We each have partial truths, and we need the continual flow of ideas such that we might find a full composite. This is an approach to the use of opposition which is totally different from defensive resistance or the avoidance of opposition. It means turning toward others rather than away from them. It means seeing others as humans having dignity and worth, having feelings and potential, and also having the capacity for self-delusion just like ourselves.

In order to be able to listen and to learn from opposing ideas and persons, we must feel secure in our own being. The understanding of our own acceptance and the acceptance of others by our Creator allows for this mutual search on behalf of all of us. The dimension of risk of failure is not excluded. That is a part of our faith as well. All things will not necessarily have happy endings, but our ultimate affirmation says that God intends to bring all peoples to Himself through His all-inclusive love and purpose. This affirmation recognizes the concept of ministry that calls us into relationships with one another whereby we can help persons or groups to change or actualize. The confrontation that Jesus makes of each of us, as well as of those whom we read about in the New Testament, is first the confrontation of accepting love and then the call toward new being and new possibilities. This induces a change which is a necessary part of life if we are going to live and grow as a follower of His. Our task in the Christian community is the delicate and sensitive one of providing helping relationships whereby people open their lives to the guidance of the Holy Spirit. Coercion or force will not do. Each must make his/her own response. What we can do is provide the helping relationship, the environment whereby the person or group has the opportunity to change and to grow toward their potential. The Christian community is that group which can provide the environment of unconditional love, assuring the self-worth and esteem necessary in the nurture of change and growth. The challenge to each within the Christian community is whether or not one can act consistently with his/her faith. The helping relationship costs in terms of time, effort, emotional energy. We are asked to willingly suffer. Each receives the challenge to this ministry of relationship because he/she believes in the potentiality residing in the relationship for the operation of the Holy Spirit. One must trust the working of the Holy Spirit in the group and in the inner workings of the other person. All the members in such a community may be recreated by the Spirit and achieve, in some measure, their God-given potentiality.

CONFLICT: A THEOLOGICAL UNDERSTANDING

Conflict, in its proper sense, is not oriented ultimately toward upheaval and destruction but toward the constructive and reconciling resolution of disruptive and divisive forces. Conflict thereby relates inseparably to both chaos and reconciliation. The disruption accompanying change often produces chaos. It is the initial stage in the experience of change. But chaos need not conclude the process. The ultimate goal includes both reconciliation and integration, but one does not get there through the process of cheap grace. One must come through the cross and reconciliation in the resolution of conflict. Conflict is a process, a means to an end. It connects the disruption and chaos of the old with the establishment of harmony and resolution of the new and not yet. Conflict is as essential to the Christian faith as is the cross. Jesus' life fulfilled the law and led to the establishment of a new order.

That meant conflict. No fulfilling change seems to come about without this movement from chaos and disorganization to resolution and reconciliation.

The utilization of the conflict process can achieve reconciliation. Conflict is thereby an appropriate theological category and can be seen as an integral part of the Christian faith and ministry. The fellowship of reconciliation emerges only through the fellowship of suffering, but that suffering has proven itself as the way to new hope. That is the message of both the resurrection experience and the experience of co-creating life and purpose with our Creator.

Notes

1. Paul Tillich, *What Is Religion?* (New York: Harper and Row, 1969), p. 33.

2. Paul Tillich, *The Courage to Be* (New Haven: Yale University Press, 1952), p. 47.

3. Richard N. Dearing, "The Theological Significance of Psychological Conflict: A Case Study in Paul Tillich" (Th. D. diss., Iliff School of Theology, 1970), pp. 305–311.

4. Ibid., p. 313.

5. Ibid., pp. 335–337.

6. John Macquarrie, *Principles of Christian Theology* (New York: Charles Scribner's Sons, 1977), pp. 62–64.

7. Paul S. Schilling, *God and Human Anguish* (Nashville: Abingdon Press, 1977), p. 50.

8. Ibid.

9. Ibid., pp. 268–274.

10. Macquarrie, *Principles of Christian Theology,* pp. 74–80.

11. Paul Tillich, "The Conception of Man in Existential Philosophy," *Journal of Religion* 19 (July 1939): 213.

12. Paul Tillich, *Systematic Theology,* vol. 3 (Chicago: University of Chicago Press, 1963), p. 27.

13. Gordon Jackson, "The Problem of Hostility: Psychologically and Theologically Considered," *Journal of Religion and Health* 11, no. 1 (1972): 79–84.

14. Ibid., p. 84.

15. Ibid., p. 85.

16. John F. Haught, *Religion and Self-Acceptance* (New York: Paulist Press, 1976), pp. 172–173.

17. Ibid., pp. 175–176.

18. Robert L. Conrad, "Creative Learning in Christian Education: A Model of Creative Conflict" (Paper given at the Association of Professors and Researchers in Religious Education meeting, Nov. 19, 1977, St. Louis, Mo.).

19. Paul Tillich, *Systematic Theology,* vol. 1 (Chicago: University of Chicago Press, 1951), pp. 193–203.

20. Dearing, "The Theological Significance of Psychological Conflict: A Case Study in Paul Tillich," pp. 291–292.

21. T. W. Ogletree, "Power and Human Fulfillment," *Pastoral Psychology* 22, no. 216 (1971): 52.

5 Conflict and Power

THE MEANINGS AND USE OF POWER

The theme of power brings ambiguous feelings to people in the church. Power carries a positive valence when reference is made to the power of love or God's power, but when it goes beyond that a negative valence pervades. Yet power is essential in any treatment of the subject of conflict. This avoidance of being open with power rests upon an understanding of power as competitive and seeking control, a power of domination by persons that is seen as unloving, unchristian, and sinful. Christian theology refers to power belonging to God alone.

A different understanding of power needs to be brought to the church and used in the educational development of our church program. This understanding is grounded in the self's basic thrust toward self-expression and self-actualization. Power in its deepest sense is not some person(s) dominating others, but all persons fulfilling their richest possibilities and God-given potential in the interaction of the human community. Power has a positive import in relation to the moral and religious grounding of our lives. It is the positive thrust in human life toward fulfillment and self-actualization. The church as an organization can play a critical role in this process.

This is not to deny that power may be gained at the cost of others, but it is to say that power can be enhanced only cooperatively. Coercive power used for domination is most costly and less likely to prevail than non-coercive power. The win/lose lifestyle is basically shortsighted.

In May of 1974, Blaine F. Hartford of the Niagara Institute of Behavioral Science wrote a paper on the meaning of power that contributes greatly to our understanding at this point. He recognizes that the individual who seeks to discover power faces the fear of violence and destruction. Power can produce a genuine sense of discomfort, leading to its categorization as evil. A negative mythology has been created around the concept of power as a result. When this negative mythology has control, then a significant impediment to growth itself forms within us.

Blaine Hartford chooses to go with a new definition in understanding power. In it he describes power in interpersonal terms as the capability of causing a change in behavior. It thereby becomes a force component of behavior. The taproot of that energy for behavior is the sense of self-worth. The strength of the negative or positive valence of the person's self-worth determines whether that person's power will be expressed constructively or destructively, or even expressed at all.[1]

This "taproot" of self-worth has become a central factor in my own understanding of the dynamics of power and conflict. Hartford has put his finger on a vital understanding for us in the church as we investigate the potential of the creative use of conflict and strive for its understanding. It was stated earlier that the intrapersonal conflict was the base for all other conflict. Out of such ambivalence within ourselves comes a projection of that inner conflict to others around us. Given our own self-understanding as having a negative self-worth, we react defensively in relationship to others and tend to strive after a win/lose process rather than a win/win process. We have a need to make others into the same image as ourselves with a negative valence. If our self-worth emerges as positive and our image, then, in relationships is one of having self-worth and value, then we can more easily project that value onto others and work with them in empowering one another toward self-actualization. We then will be more likely to handle conflict and power dynamics in a constructive way rather than destructive. A positive sense of self-worth creates a constructive power base for behavior which enables a person to influence his/her own behavior as well as that of others in the pursuit of basic goals.

As we look at this power dynamic in relationships between individuals, the positive sense of self-worth finds support by what Hartford calls transactional equilibrium, or the "continual behavioral adjustments of each individual in a transactional exchange aimed at maintaining a sense of felt equality of power with the transactional partner."[2] This reciprocity of power maintains individual security as the individual relates to others.

There is an important concept here. Power is viewed in terms of potency. We need to understand power on the one hand as having an unusually high degree of potency, or force, and on the other extreme as having a low degree of impotence, the state of powerlessness or helplessness. This understanding of power sees it as either actualized or latent. Power actualized is power resultant in behavior toward the goal of the individual or group, and power described as latent is a power which lies in the unconscious, withheld from behavior. Growth in the individual, then, may be seen as transferring power potential from latency to actualization.[3]

Actualized power embodies a synthesis of either organic or vested power. Organic power emanates from the physiological realm of the individual and vested power comes from within the organizational realm in some specific role enacted. The expression of power in either organic or vested form by individual or group translates from latent to actualized power.

Power, then, represents our attempt to enforce our values, and when those values are in conflict themselves, a tremendous sense of ambivalence and threat follows. We can become paralyzed with our own growth and progress and find frustration as our major emotional expression. This oppositional expression within is projected without, and we enter vehemently into a win/lose style. We enter into competition with others as we are competitive with our diverse drives within. We need to prove ourselves over against another. It can come down to a matter of personal survival.

This opposes the concept of collaboration which pulls together the power of individuals for the intent of maximizing the achievement of our mutually desired ends and goals. This win/win lifestyle depends upon the inner state of the individual. The individual needs to feel the capability of actualizing his/her own power with the corresponding enhancement of his/her own self-worth. If we become too dependent on others for self-worth, we find that this tends to foster continuing competitiveness in a sense of self over against other.

A goal which Hartford sets for the integration of power within an individual is to find the interdependent relationship in which a person overcomes the fear of losing power and is able to commit energies to an intimate relationship (within self and with others) with the full confidence of self-integrity and ownership. This calls for a good sense of self-worth to free the energies for a healthy collaboration that is not too dependent upon another, but yet is free from the threat by the other.[5] The key to notice again is the positive or negative balance of the sense of self-worth.

This basic theory on power is pursued further by T. W.

Ogletree in his article, "Power and Human Fulfillment." In this article he makes reference to a study made by Harold Lasswell in his book, *Power and Personality* (New York: W. W. Norton, 1948). Lasswell's study indicates that persons who have unusually high power drives are characteristically insecure and uncertain of their own worth. They compensate for this inadequacy by attempting to dominate others. They need to control in order to satisfy a basic need for self-worth and power. The stronger person can let others be to call forth their own creative possibilities. The study concludes that such insecure persons cannot be good leaders, for their need to dominate makes them ineffective.[6]

Power that is used for selfish ends of domination and control leads to a distorted form of self-affirmation. Power becomes a tool to compensate for our limitations that we feel as a human being. Tillich sees it as our anxiety resulting from the facing of our nothingness. Reinhold Niebuhr sees it as our struggle for the moral use of power as a part of acting out our nature as human beings. Power, as dominance and control, cannot overcome the feeling of brokenness in the human community that results from its distorted use. The fundamental need for self-worth does not get satisfied in this use of power. The power drive has deep roots in our fundamental human need for self-worth, for significance, for self-esteem. If we use it as a distorted form of self-affirmation, then we are merely striving to compensate for our feeling of being strung between our potential and our limits. This view of power in terms of domination and control, akin to Niebuhr's view of power as man's sin, does not show the more positive definition and use of power as that which moves us toward self-actualization.

Power should not be seen, therefore, as merely a force toward gaining personal advantage or getting one's own way. It is more fruitful to view power as the mobilization of one's own life resources in the developing unity of one's own being. As mentioned before, power links one to the fulfillment of one's potential. In fact, Ogletree maintains that power is not goal attainment. It is an "unending process involving ever-new actualizations."[7] As the changing self continues to reach specific points of actualization, there is then an ever increasing need to go further. The process becomes an essentially unfinishable task of the human being.

Ogletree contributes yet further with two criteria used to measure power: 1) we have more power the more we can bring all aspects of our being positively into play, and 2) we have more power the more the various dynamics of our being are working in some creative unity. In sum, the more unified our life, the less energy wasted with internal conflict.[8]

In order to accomplish this end of a unified life, we need to creatively appropriate our human limitations. Instead of fighting to compensate for them, we need to move toward the embrace of our whole life, even its demonic, in order to be completely actualized. This is why self-acceptance is a crucial feature in understanding the creative use of power. Power must help us get in touch with all of our life and utilize it in ever new forms of self-creation and expression. In the encounter with others who are also trying to realize their fulfillment, we may find blocks to our progress and provide blocks to others. We do this only when we find ourself threatened by our encounter and its resultant frustration. The very difference between persons which creates the threatening experience can also provide the very possibility present when our differences are utilized together for our mutual potential. If our basic self-worth allows, we can move toward transformation and enrichment in a manner that could not have happened apart from the encounter with others who are different from ourselves.

Our own actualized power cannot, then, be treated solely

in terms of actualization and unification of our individual life resources. Others become critical to the fulfillment of our potentialities. It is at this point that the Christian community comes into its own as the environment for the helping ministry, as each works with the other as catalyst and contributor in working out not only one's own, but also the other's potentialities. The power of this caring community whose individuals have self-esteem from the basic fact of their acceptance by God and by one another is an unrealized resource within the church. If we believe, with Ogletree, that the fullest development of a person's power of being resides in the creative interaction with fellow human beings, the Christian community could become a force to be reckoned with in the creative use of conflict toward our self-actualization. It is critical to view power here as an ever growing resource, waiting for its utilization, rather than a scarce commodity for which we must compete. Our church leadership must find the way to effectively mobilize this resource within the Christian community in response to Christ's call to all of us to fulfill our larger call to God and to another. In this form of community, leadership need not be concerned about the power of dominance and control, but rather the power to maximize resource development of all in the pursuit of common, compatible goals.

Ogletree calls our attention to the meaning of divine power in the New Testament. That power does not emerge as a tyrant who does whatever he pleases. Rather, we see a God who discloses Himself as an inexhaustible resource for the realization of forms of life in creation which are to be a part of His plan. The self-actualization of God's own creation is a part of the fulfillment of His own being. This kind of God is an enabling, empowering presence that energizes His creation toward its own fulfillment.[9] The Christian community must grow into a place where this dynamic can be worked out. Parts II and III of this book will hopefully aid in the creative use of the potential of the Christian community through conflict.

The maximum development of power in a social setting does not necessarily consist of some person or group imposing its will on the whole. Such action demands too much energy to maintain control and it blankets other talents and potentialities within. Maximum development consists in rallying all the resources of groups toward their common goals. If all are aware of their common interest, motivation will be there to invest themselves toward common goals. Talcott Parsons calls this the "collective effectiveness," the ability of persons in leadership to mobilize the resources of the group or organizations in society in pursuit of their common social goals.[10] The fullest development of our individual aim, corporate power, resides in our creative relationships with one another, allowing the best in each to be given toward the common good. This places power out of the concept of a scarce commodity for which we all are in competition. It does place it as an expansive dynamic which can be released for the good of all. We in the church have a tremendous potential to work with the empowering presence of God to energize our life possibilities within the context of the Christian community and outward to the whole of the human community.

CONFLICT AS POWER FOR MINISTRY

Conflict as chaos has been one of the images which has kept the church from the utilization of this power dynamic. The fear of power as control and dominance and the conviction that it has no place in the loving community has kept power as an immobilizing image in the church. As a result, the church has been criticized as a loving community that does not know how to act or to move with any intentional force. The people of the church need to be moved from this inactivity and fear to focus on utilization of power toward common goals and issues. Once movement is made to get hold of specific issues and to will to do something about them, there can be a new feeling of power in the Christian community. The focus on the common goal and the compromise or negotiation necessary to move toward that goal constitute an empowering act. Power develops into the engagement in intentional business and not into disruptive activity. Conflict thus becomes the dynamic which empowers the people. The conflict raises the issues, clarifies and establishes goals. In this sense, conflict empowers the people to move toward the fulfillment of self and community. Conflict can be the means of overcoming the sense of powerlessness, complacency, and apathy which can deaden individuals and communities. A real need exists in the church to rediscover power in this positive sense. It does require a faith that chaos, anger, confusion, and doubt can be overcome and that conflict can bring the church toward reconciliation and new possibilities.

An important distinction should be offered at this time between individual power and group power. Rensis and Jane Likert have been helpful in making this distinction. They distinguish between negative power and positive power for the individual. Positive power for the individual can be such as reward power, legitimate power, referent power, and expert power. The negative concept of power consists mostly of coercive, and possibly some expert power. Informational power can also be used negatively as well as positively, but this description has most to do with person-to-person interaction.[11] There is no use made of the power of the group. Group power brings us to a whole new level of influence, quite different from the individual negative and positive use. The strength of group power comes from the desire of individuals to achieve and maintain a sense of personal worth and importance. This goes back to our earlier concept of the need for self-worth and self-esteem in all of us as a determining point for how we will utilize, or manage, conflict. This need for personal worth is a creative force that helps individuals seek membership in groups whose values are consistent with theirs, and motivates them to want to be valued by this group or groups. Strong forces exist within an individual to engage in behavior toward achieving the goals of the group, since the group values this behavior. It is called group power. With this group power, each person can influence others because they are members of the same group. The capacity varies, but it is still strong for all, and reciprocal in character. Group power is not as threatening as individual power. An increase in group power does not benefit one party at the expense of another. Neither party need fear an increase in the strength of group power. This is not the case with individual power. Group power gives an increasing sense of a win/win situation by all, and leads to the development of a mutually acceptable solution. This cooperative behavior achieves better results than the competitive win/lose situation which individuals usually get into, since it creates a greater total coordinated motivational force. The source again, we should note, is a desire of all to achieve and maintain a sense of personal worth and importance. The group with the common goals provides this opportunity. In conflict situations, the shift from using power over others (win/lose) to using a cooperative, joint power with others (win/win) is an important change in the strategy of resolution. Issues are clarified and brought to consciousness at low risk level, diversity becomes a power toward common good rather than separate evil, and the motivating force of the individual toward self-worth and the realization of the group goals gives a power potential in cooperative form that can move any organization to heights of accomplishment.

Conflict as power for ministry has been given major impetus by the writing and work of Lyle Schaller. His book, *Community Organization: Conflict and Reconciliation,* has given a strong activistic image to the power potential of the church in the community. The church as a power base in the community has been very threatening to both those within the church and without it. There is good reason to fear the potential of power being corrupted. What starts out as an expression of God's love of justice for his creation can turn toward an end in itself. The power of the church through community organization can be an effective mobilization of the force of love for justice, as well as for personal gain and power for its own sake. Community organization, in its best sense, empowers people to grow and gain a new dignity to become effective participants in the decision-making processes which affect their lives. It helps people to come closer to developing the potential which has been created within them. It need not be self-centered, but rather centered in the love of neighbor and self.[12] Schaller contends that the church's primary motive for being involved in community organization is for human resource development, not the effecting of social change. The latter may be necessary toward the fostering of human resource development. Community organization does deal with the possibility of the creation of new centers of power which may be necessary in order to achieve the ends aforementioned. Fear holds us back, making us reluctant to give approval to conflict because of our recognition of the ease with which it turns into violence, destruction, and disruption of the public order. On the other hand, there is tremendous excitement in the possibilities of the motivation toward power and conflict. Schaller does recommend that one try the personal, direct, cooperative approach first, but if that fails, then there is justification to move toward the pressure of tension and community organization.[13]

Paul Tournier sheds some light on this grey area of violence and power which has so troubled the Christian community. He seems to agree with Lyle Schaller's concern for aggressive action when necessary. Tournier attempts to distinguish between two types of violence. He labels one a benign violence which is put to the service of others, protecting the weak, liberating the exploited, healing the sick, fighting injustice. The other forms of violence he labels improper violence, which one carries out on one's own behalf, aimed at securing power for one's own sake. The latter violence appears inspired by the fascination of power or by a need for higher self-esteem and worth. The distinction between benign and improper violence reflects a previous theological battle between the divine and human will—the battle as to whether to serve God and humanity or the self.[14]

The model for Schaller is Saul Alinsky's *Community Organization* and his philosophy and purpose as the redistribution of power in the community. Alinsky's process polarizes the community, which many feel inhibits the dynamics of problem solving. The polar method identifies and attacks the enemy. Bonds of a common front result. A major criticism of the Alinsky approach as described is theological. Ends become justified over means. The issue focuses on the use of force, polarity, fear, and hostility to win allegiance in the establishment of power. That power directs the redistribution of power, moving toward social justice and the help of those who are unable to fulfill themselves in the present organization. This has been distasteful to the church.

In summary, power has a positive valence when it is seen

as the ability to influence the actions and decisions of others toward common valued goals. Power already pervades the church. It needs to be brought to consciousness and intentional use as a part of the process of community organization. Lyle Schaller offers some valuable observations on power relevant to the process of community organization which could be helpful to the church person. He lists the following:

1. There is an important distinction between power and authority. There is delegated power in the positions of authority, and this is a legitimate possession of power. Others, without this vested power, may also hold power by sanctions which can influence decision making. This does create the possibility of conflict between authority and informal power.
2. There is often a distinction between power and leadership. One can prepare persons for leadership and help them to acquire power.
3. The exercise of power is determined by values and relationships. Power can fluctuate on the changes of relationships or values. The power to coerce may or may not be a part of the value system for relationships.
4. The concept of a single community power structure is a myth. Many power centers are existent in a community. Coalitions can vary greatly, as well.
5. Power is necessary for anyone seeking to participate in the community decision-making process.
6. Authority can be granted or given, but power must be earned. Authority gives some power, but power does separate from authority and is earned.
7. There are many sources of power. Organization is one. Knowledge is another. Charisma, possessions, convictions, birth, and conflict are all sources of power.

8. The easiest power to acquire is the power of veto. The hardest to acquire is the power to initiate and implement.

9. The established holders of power generally prefer cooperation to conflict because conflict is disruptive and threatening. Holders of power usually give up more to the threat of power than to the actual use of power.

10. The extent of power generally is overestimated. People usually attribute to others more power than they do, in fact, possess.

11. The distinction between the overt use of power and covert use of power is underemphasized. Doing nothing, or foot-dragging, is power in resistance to change.

12. The acquisition and the possession of power often does change the powerholder.

13. Concentration on the acquisition of power can thwart human resource development as the positive force of community organization.[15]

Theologically, Schaller does recognize Reinhold Niebuhr's theology about the nature of man and power. Power should be a means to an end, never an end in itself. When power is sought it is often sought as a corrupting force and not a moral one, creating the sinful nature of humanity. This should not be a determining factor in avoiding power and its positive use and gain for persons and society. Schaller affirms with others that the Christian can act with the use of non-violent conflict without the danger of degenerating to violence if the person acts in the spirit of reconciliation. An equilibrium can be brought to the battle with conflict and violence by meditation and reflection. Pausing to recognize the sovereignty of God and our own need for God's acceptance of us as we are can bring a wisdom for action that may well be missing without such reflection. Conflict and reconciliation are not incompatible. Not all conflict is necessary and there is need to minimize unnecessary conflict. The ministry of reconciliation is for all, however, the rich and the poor, and all must be involved in the ministry to the alienated of our society. The primary purpose of community organization for Schaller is to help individuals develop and use the resources God has given them, enabling the individual to control his/her own destiny and the destiny of the community. The unique task of the church is to add to this process of community change and organization the dimension of love, justice, redemption, reconciliation, mercy, and the judgment of God.[16] Power evokes potential without direction, and because of this, we can simultaneously be excited by its possibilities for creativity and yet disturbed by the possibilities for harm. Power has been viewed here as an instrument for the achievement of personal goals, with both positive and negative valence, as well as the use to achieve collective goals for the good of individuals and the group as a whole. There seems to be a need for both a faith and an understanding, as well as a training for the use of power in order to avoid the threatening aspects and to emphasize the positive gain for the use of power in conflict. Paul Tournier seeks this harmony between power and love, using the analogy of the right and left hands of God. Such harmony is possible by admitting to the presence and validity of power, but placing it in the right hand of God and not our own. We must recognize the need for the other hand of God. That left hand symbolizes love. Poetically, we may move from God's right hand to the left, gathered in by that love. We need to put these two hands together as our own—in prayer and faith, affirming both power and love brought together in meditation and reflection for equilibrium.[17]

Power can be used either in the process of attempting to

influence the choices of authorities in structure and organization, or to describe the process that authorities use as they attempt to achieve collective goals and maintain legitimacy. Both uses of power are found within the church organization. They need to be understood to utilize the conflict dynamic. The meaning and use of this power is yet a vital question for the church as an intentional community to answer. Depending on how the issue of power is worked through, the vitality and creative possibility of the church as a Christian community will be decided. Power, like conflict, is already present. The question is its recognition, its understanding, and its utilization. To this end, I hope this book will be useful.

Notes

1. Blaine F. Hartford, "A Meaning of Power" (Niagara, New York: Niagara Institute of Behavioral Science, 1974), pp. 1-3.

2. Ibid., p. 4.

3. Ibid., p. 5.

4. Ibid., p. 6.

5. Ibid., p. 12.

6. T. W. Ogletree, "Power and Human Fulfillment," *Pastoral Psychology* 22, no. 216 (1971): 47.

7. Ibid., p. 47.

8. Ibid., p. 48.

9. Ibid., p. 52.

10. Talcott Parsons, "On the Concept of Political Power," in *Politics and Social Structure* (New York: Free Press, 1969), pp. 360-362.

11. Rensis and Jane Likert, *New Ways of Managing Conflict* (New York: McGraw-Hill, 1976), pp. 269-282.

12. Lyle E. Schaller, *Community Organization: Conflict and Reconciliation* (Nashville: Abingdon Press, 1966), pp. 24-25.

13. Ibid., p. 89.

14. Paul Tournier, *The Violence Within* (New York: Harper and Row, 1977), p. 113.

15. Schaller, *Community Organization: Conflict and Reconciliation*, pp. 117-126.

16. Ibid., pp. 132-138.

17. Tournier, *The Violence Within*, pp. 190-195.

6 Conflict and Church Growth

Some people are asking the question whether or not the institution of the church will be able to carry its goals into the future as it now is. Can the church play its missional role as reconciler, or will it just be a part of the problem of society? The church seems to be hampered by some myths in the carrying out of its goals and mission. M. C. Hendrickson gives us a list of such myths that he sees standing in the way of the church and its mission.

1. Conflict which disrupts the peace in the church and the family is demonic.
2. A loving person is one who is always tranquil, stable, and serene.
3. Administration, worship, and program forms in the church are established and not subject to change.
4. Spiritualizing the individual believer and the church is the aim and goal.
5. America, as the promised land, and our governmental form, is tantamount to God's kingdom.[1]

These may sound overstated, but for many these myths have the appearance of reality. As a result, the church responds to conflict by withdrawing from it. Tactics of repression are needed in order to avoid obvious conflict possibilities.

These myths ignore the possibility of growth based on conflict. They lead people to feel that the acceptance and use of it cannot be tolerated in looking to the future of the church. However, just possibly the loving person may in fact demand conflict to be truly loving. Rigidity of administration, worship, and program is necessary for many to feel secure in the bastion of the church which protects them from change. The spiritualization task of the church, focused upon the individual, tends to leave out the world and the church's responsibility for it. Justifying such individual spiritualization seems to be the basic mission, establishing the love affair between the person and God. The repression of conflict, which is necessary in order to hold the church to such myths, requires great energy. Rugged individualism and personal moralism become major values, discouraging any sensitivity to diversity and its use for good and growth. Such attitudes allow little understanding of each person as a child of God.

COURAGE FOR CHANGE

I believe it is fairly evident now that change in the local church is no longer an option. It is a necessity. The capabilities are there just as they are for any living organism. With such radical change going on in the society around us, creative institutions are going to have to discover how they can relate meaningfully to such flow. It has been said of the Holy Spirit that it has the potential to make all things new. That potential may hardly be used in the church without some intentional understanding of the meaning of change and conflict for the church's mission. If the church is to maintain its role of being a part of God's mission in the world, there must be some courageous movement to act as a disciple amidst God's original and continuing creation. The church cannot be found as a captive of the social and cultural situation around it. This does not mean retreating from the world, but rather confronting the world, utilizing what strengths that it has to move with confidence through the surrounding change in which it must live. An example of the strength of this kind of spirit in the church has been given by Harold R. Fray, Jr., in his description of the journey of the Eliot Church of Newton, Massachusetts, in his book, *Conflict and Change in the Church*. Fray understands that the world shapes the ministry of the church, and it is the church's action in relation to that world that gives reality and substance to the church's mission. The process is quite risky, but also quite necessary.[2]

Any time this type of mission of the church is taken seriously, you can be sure that conflict will be a part of the experience. It cannot be otherwise, for church members were not intended to be consumers or spiritual mendicants, but rather disciples of Christ. The members are not consumers of religion, nor an end in themselves, but exist as the church for the sake of being able to participate in God's mission with the world.[3] This requires flexibility of form and an anticipation of the risks of change. Faith and the vitality of worship become important ingredients if one is to take on this mission and become enabled to respond. Such existence as described here involves the participants in constant decision making. This decision making lays the groundwork for conflict and its utilization in the church's mission. Change finds its roots in confrontation and decision making.

Conflict has not been totally accepted as a valued portion of the mission of the church because the church often experiences it as disintegrating, dysfunctional, and dissociating. Symptoms of this type of conflict have been described by Speed Leas and Paul Kittlaus. The symptoms observed are:

internal division, organization of cliques, the increased use of voting for decision making, long, unfulfilling meetings, decreasing attendance, increased use of hostile language, the imaging of others as the enemy, and fear out of control. The results of such conflict show a win/lose lifestyle: the feeling of conspiracies, incongruity of public versus private statements, unfocused anxiety and anger, displacement of hostility with acting out, mistrust, loss of income and membership, as well as painful pressure on ministerial staff.[4]

Such poor management and appreciation of conflict was the reason why Leas and Kittlaus wrote their book. Their goal was to help the church accomplish its mission through the managing of conflict already present.

The type of church which would respond best to conflict management and utilization, according to Leas and Kittlaus, is one described as the pluralistic community. In it the membership is very diverse, calling for reconciliation in the internal dynamics of the congregation. In order to minister to everyone, it would be vital for the leaders to understand interpersonal and intergroup conflict management. The potential within would be great for individual fulfillment as well as missional fulfillment. This typology is quite opposite from that described as the sheltered community in which the membership is most homogeneous, living easily and comfortably together.[5] Conflict experienced in the pluralistic type church can be a positive experience. Leas and Kittlaus have listed four major areas where conflict does play an essentially positive role. They list the following:

1. Empowerment—an energizing and strengthening process for group life. Too much can be immobilizing. However, some conflict can move a group from an apathetic state into a newly energized group.
2. Established identity—boundary lines are formed versus

the outsiders. It is strengthening to a group to come to determine who they are.

3. Unifying the in group—conflict plays down the differences within and forces them to become more effective as a task group.

4. Bearing the intolerable—conflict can make one aware of the limits of strength and help make liveable the conflict by accepting the situation as it is experienced. One cannot know that without having experienced the conflict.[6]

The church experiences these functions of conflict either as a whole or as smaller groups within the congregation. This positive functioning of conflict is not to cover over the possibility that conflict can go awry and become destructive and violent. This is a particular reason why we need to understand conflict dynamics and learn skills in managing and utilizing this force for the church.

GROUP THINK

Based upon the concept of conflict as demonic and the desire to repress and avoid it, a phenomenon can occur within the church that has been named "group think." Sociologist Irving Janis has coined this phrase. It is descriptive of a drive for consensus at the cost of realistic consideration of alternative ideas. Individuals tend to suppress themselves in such groups in order to allow the group to reach an agreement quickly without turmoil. It is not forced, but a voluntary action. Conflict does not have time to develop because of the rush for an early conclusion. Several symptoms of "group think" have been outlined as follows:

1. There is a strong feeling of cohesion of group members' points of view, whether real or not. The cohesion of the group is both a result and a cause of majority opinions. Dissenters are not argued with, but merely ignored.
2. There is a belief in group invulnerability. Decisions that are made in the group cannot be wrong.
3. Rationalization is characteristic of "group think." It minimizes evidence to the contrary of decisions and plans that have been made.
4. There is a development and promotion of negative stereotypes of outsiders.

Correctives are needed in order to avoid "group think" in the church, especially as it is so adaptable to the situation of the church. Corrections need to be applied early in the group life, however, to be effective. Such corrections could be as follows:

1. The group must be kept free from undue influences from different status levels of group members.
2. Methods of obtaining information that challenge prevailing or gathering wisdom of the group must be found. There can be no selective inattention.
3. From the beginning, a norm must be developed that makes disagreement acceptable in discussion.
4. The use of the devil's advocate may be necessary in order to keep the group free from a sense of invulnerability.[7]

INDICES OF CHANGE

The attempts to cover over conflict, by "group think" or any other process, are made by both clergy and laity. Intelligent leaders, either professional or lay, have been accused of running through many a red light that should have been an indication that conflict was present but not recognized. There are a few indices that should give any of us an idea of a change in the tension level. Simple indicators to be used in the church may be as follows. These are listed in order of increasing danger:

1. Voting patterns indicating the rise of opposition to leadership
2. Direct protest of a policy or a decision
3. Change in attendance at meetings
4. Change in revenue
5. A persisting issue of abrasive quality that just won't be settled
6. The withdrawal of support by some of the power structure
7. An increase in polarization
8. The withdrawal of key persons or groups from communication[8]

These simple indices could be valuable for clergy and lay leadership to watch for in their congregation.

CHURCH AS MINI-CULTURE

Another helpful concept for the church leadership to keep in mind is the understanding of the congregation as a miniature culture. Many precedents are built up which are just like the development of a social culture. When the elements of a culture are ignored by new leadership, then conflict is unnecessarily encountered. New leadership, such as a new pastor or new lay leadership, needs to be very much aware of that particular culture which they have inherited. The previously cited indices of discontent are a way of viewing whether or not that culture is being violated.

I think it valuable to describe what is meant by the congregation as a miniature culture. The following elements need to be understood in relation to a particular congregation:

1. Custom and stability. The status quo demands defense because of the need to preserve the security of custom. Outsiders threaten that order and must take time to be acculturated.

2. Structure. All groups and societies have at least two boundaries, an external and an internal one. These must be preserved in order to maintain group identity. Power and status are very much involved in the group structure. Any attempt to change these factors will meet with strong opposition.

3. Time. Time must be used effectively without fighting it. Attempts to revise systems or cultures must be projected in the long range, not the very short range. Timing is an important skill for leadership to learn.

4. Reward and punishment. Rewards in cultures and groups go to those who conform, and punishment goes to those who attempt to threaten and change too fast. There is a vital balance, or tension, over this process. A sense of strain and anxiety becomes the punishment of those who deviate.

5. A sense of strain. Imbalances between different goals and imbalance between individual costs and rewards produce this tension. When there are anxiety and strain, there had better be adequate hope of reward in order for members to face and tolerate the strain. Goals pull an organization beyond the status quo creating the anxiety.

6. Growth and conflict. Between the yearning for stability and the drive for achievement, there is an aim for growth and self-realization. Growth may be experienced as the creative possibilities from the cost of strain. The energies of conflict must be constructively mobilized in order to gain the positive end of growth.

7. Emotional bonds. These bonds hold the culture or organization together through certain roles. A person's gains and losses are expressed emotionally. We understand that in a positive sense. We have trouble with the negative expression. Emotional attachments develop between members and with leaders. This determines much of the character and purpose of the culture and group.

8. Rationality. Rational leaders in a culture or the church must be able to admit their own emotions as well as those of others. We must be aware of how self-centeredness and self-needs block our pure rationality and good will. Rather than deny such emotions, rational leadership must admit them in self and others and learn how to live in such interrelationship without losing either humanity or rationality.[9]

If leadership in the church can remember the church as a culture and its various components, the process of exerting leadership and of utilizing potential conflict will be easier, as well as creative, rather than merely stressful.

In connection with the latter point of rationality, it is important for persons in leadership to make a decision as to their assumptions about behavior of men and women. If the leadership has the theory that people are only motivated by their basic needs for security and survival, then that leadership will concentrate power and control with heavy emphasis on direction and coercion. Development of an elite within the church or group becomes justified on the basis of effectiveness and the good of the whole. If, on the other hand, leadership accepts a theory about behavior which admits to material and security needs but then allows for both work and play as an acceptable natural part of human behavior, that leadership will take a totally different form. This theory assumes that persons will exercise self-control and self-direction and can be trusted because of such commitment. Rewards motivate and are associated with their achievement. Persons can accept and do seek responsibility. This leads to the possibility of creative achievement in organizations by persons at all levels of the structure. Lay leadership and training becomes crucial for the church. Conflict management and utilization as discussed in this book assumes the latter theory. The assumption was made earlier and is now repeated that there is no question about the presence of diversity in most of our churches. The question is, rather, how will that diversity be utilized?

THE CHURCH ALIVE

Where the church is alive, it must deal with conflict. Both church members and ministers do get excited about their work and can naturally stir up diversity and controversy. How the church deals with this will determine whether it is productive and creative, or counterproductive and destructive to its sense of mission. The resultant conflict can alienate and block effective work as well as clarify and broaden understanding of important issues, thereby becoming a source of motivation and a release of new energy. The missing ingredient is often the sense of understanding and skills that are necessary to utilize this force to its positive end.

Paul, in his writings in Romans 8, gives us a sense of the sin of the flesh as well as the hope of the spirit. The possibility for creativity and glory amid suffering is the very hope that is needed to move through the chaos of conflict into the future of reconciliation and new-being. In Paul's letter to the Ephesians, in the 4th chapter, he allows for the possibility of one to be angry and yet sin not. Differences of opinion do not violate the spirit of the Gospel, and in fact, may be necessary in order to carry out that spirit. We certainly inherited conflict at our roots, noted as one reads through the Old Testament passages. Jesus' ministry certainly carries it into the New Testament. In fact, it was Jesus who made the statement that he had come not to bring peace, but a sword. Jesus utilized conflict as a means of interpreting and carrying out his ministry.

The church could grow in strength for its mission if it would take the risk of utilizing conflict in ways such as prepared by Charles P. Jaeger in his *Utilizing Conflict: A Learning System.* Programs such as this will help clergy and lay persons to understand the dynamics of conflict and learn some skills as to how to work with it. This program will be outlined in greater detail as we deal with specific procedures for using creative conflict in the church. The church must be able to deal with such barriers as fearing disruption of its order, fearing a worsening of what they see to be a conflicting situation coming, fearing personal vulnerability, the loss of tradition, the changing of group norms, and power differences. The church stands to gain the following: 1) a greater diversity of viewpoints than have been heard before, 2) innovative and creative ideas for the church and its mission, 3) clearer communication as to each person's positions and views, 4) new motivation and energy, 5) a greater sense of genuineness in personal relationships, and 6) increased commitment to both task and relationship in the church.[10]

ACCEPTANCE AND ORGANIZATIONAL DEVELOPMENT

The subject of self-acceptance was raised in the chapter on psychological dynamics of conflict. Its importance has been seen by theorists as well as those who are working out the design of organizational processes for various segments of society. Rensis and Jane Likert have written for the business and industrial sector and have something vital to say to the church in respect to the church's concern for conflict and organizational growth. Their writing has a good basis in research, particularly that research done in a psychological community. One of their discoveries from research indicates to us that the greater amount of supportive behavior contributes to a greater success in resolving conflicts constructively and achieving effective integration. Also, confrontation in dealing with conflict has helped higher-performing organizations. Therefore, they indicate supportive relationships to be critical. These are often based on the leader's behavior. Supportive behavior is vital in order that each member will view the experience that he/she is having as positive, one which will build and maintain the member's sense of personal worth and importance.[11] The importance of self-worth and self-esteem arises again for the church to be aware of as a ground base for its work with conflict. This should be no surprise to the church if it understands its theological base.

This lifts up for our review again the need to be aware of patterns of inter-relationship which have been referred to earlier as win/lose and win/win varieties. For the most part, church growth in its dealing with conflict will not occur if we allow ourselves to be forced into the win/lose pattern. Even with that pattern, some growth can occur, but it is certainly balanced by greater loss.

The win/lose pattern, in review, begins with the establishment of sides and the closing of ranks against each other. Group cohesion grows, leadership becomes concentrated with power and control, diversity is snuffed out, and the group moves quickly toward concentration of opinion and unanimity. The subjugation of differences in each group lays the groundwork for future internal strife. Groups become judgmental and perceptual distortions become greater and greater. A sense of self-superiority develops, and a stereotyping of others places them in an inferior position automatically. Distortions continue to develop in the process in both intellectual and perceptual processes. Differences are remembered, similarities are overlooked, and desire to understand another position deteriorates quickly. The pressure finally is not to be objective or innovative, or seek the best solution, but to win at any cost.[12] The winning group becomes fat and happy, and the defeated group usually has internal fighting and a shift in power status. The win/lose disagreement is really not resolved. A temporary winner emerges. Emotional responses continue and have a deteriorating effect on the whole organization.

Why do we get into the win/lose pattern? There are two basic motives at work: 1) the desire for physical security, and 2) the desire to achieve and maintain a sense of personal worth and importance. When such are threatened, intense emotional reactions follow.[13] Acceptance is noticeably missing.

Organizational development shows surprising psychological and theological insight, such as the Liker's proposal of System 4T. It has a growth orientation based upon supportive leadership. The church and clergy should take notice. Basically, leadership shows a friendly, supportive style, paying avid attention to what is said and listening to the problems of personnel. Team building facilitates the exchange of ideas and opinions at all levels. A strong goal emphasis encourages the best efforts and maintains the highest standards. The leader has an important role to help with the work of the personnel. Leaders help in planning and organization, offering new ideas and solutions to problems. They provide a strong sense of support for all concerned. The climate includes good communication flow, high involvement in decision making, a basic concern and care for persons, good management of resources, and *acceptance* of differences and disagreements and time taken to work these through.[14] If we applied such basic organizational development to the church, the church might discover that it has strong sociological, psychological, and theological bases that should promote growth and strengthening factors in this development. The support for members in their need for a sense of personal worth and importance is both a leader role and a member role. It should be noted that the Likerts feel that the System 4T that they have been describing is even more marked in its success in voluntary organizations such as the church than it is in business.

Supportive relationships are fundamental for resolving differences in conflict. The lack of such relations leads one inevitably to a win/lose strategy in which others are put down. Leadership must apply the principle of support to all, especially to those who differ, in order to move toward a win/win situation. This does not mean that a win/win situation keeps all people in harmony. We must remember that there is no real evidence that a completely harmonious context is most productive for problem solving or creativity or growth. Some degree of competition seems to help. When that competition and diversity occurs in a supportive climate, then it contributes to creative problem solving. The competition, however, must move toward collaboration. Some realism and awareness must be kept in the mind of leadership as to what limits there are for toleration of conflict. When listening and supportive behavior disappears in the exchange of diverse opinion, then the climate has changed from creative problem solving to the beginnings of a win/lose situation.

The constructive resolution of conflict finds its basis in the use of integrative goals, common values, and mutual interests. If the focus is here, then the organization finds empowerment and growth. If the focus is on integrative goals, the organization discovers that the deep-seated needs and desires of conflicting parties are brought together toward a mutually acceptable solution. Without the opportunity to participate with deep commitment to objectives, there will be little sacrifice of personal well-being for that of the organization and its mission. These basic human needs referred to are important to the success of integrative goals. These needs must be stated explicitly by the leadership so that all fully understand them. These needs include a sense of personal worth and importance, achievement, fulfillment, recognition, and self-actualization.[15]

The focus on these integrative goals leads us toward consensus-making behavior. This means that our focus is on an outcome which will be satisfying to all parties concerned. Consensus is an essential part of each step in the process. This does not mean that the conclusion will be the exact wishes of all members, but it will not violate the deep concerns of anyone and can be agreed upon by all. Unacceptable solutions are not forced upon losers, such as the usual process of church meetings that focus on Robert's Rules of Order. This widely used order is basically a win/lose situation. The basis for consensus making includes a leader who can provide orderly group problem solving, undertaken in a supportive atmosphere. If full consensus is not possible, then pragmatic consensus can be used to move toward giving a particular solution a trial run for a period of time, followed by evaluation. Growth can come from such pragmatic consensus as well as full consensus. Partial success can build trust and confidence to work toward greater success.

Pastors, as leaders, need to be particularly aware of a problem in this growth-oriented, problem-solving process. Hierarchical status can act as a strong deterrent toward involvement of membership. Many pastors act unaware of this impact. It seems the more that leaders strive for status, the more membership turns to competition and the creating of hostile relationships. This basic concern for de-emphasizing status and de-personalizing problem solving applies also to lay leadership in the church. If lay leaders exhibit a concern for status, and if they attempt to personalize issues and to involve personality differences, open communication will be critically affected and the willingness of membership to be involved and to speak up will be limited, resulting in more negative reaction. Concern for an open flow of relevant facts will be a positive contribution. It is important to understand that people do act on the basis of what they perceive the situation to be, or the facts to be, whether accurate or not. Facts must be cooperatively gathered and shared. The possibility of creative solution in problem solving is greatly enhanced when all parties carry out each step of the problem-solving process. Sometimes a third party helps this to be accomplished. If multiple groups are necessary in problem solving, it becomes important to have linked membership such that some representation is held on various groups to allow for a communication flow between groups.[16]

In summary, organizational development infers that if growth is to occur, basic human need for personal worth and importance must be at the center. Cooperation through win/win behavior patterns achieves much better results than competition in the win/lose pattern since the former creates greater total coordinated motivational forces toward growth. The movement from using power over others to using joint power with others represents an extremely fundamental factor in the strategy of resolving conflicts. It also moves us strongly toward the concept we know so well in the church called reconciliation.

RECONCILIATION

A growth orientation to the organization of the church must include conflict as inseparably related to both reconciliation and chaos. Any change in a secure environment usually introduces some disruption and chaos. Constructive and reconciling resolution is a key to both individual and organizational growth in the church. Church leadership, both lay and clergy, must be able to lead in such resolution for growth. Reconciliation is an ultimate goal in the church. It does not come cheaply, but rather comes through the symbol given to us by Christ on the cross. Suffering may well be a part of reconciliation, and conflict utilization provides us a process toward that end. It provides a connection between the disruption and chaos of the old and the movement toward the establishment of a harmonic resolution of the new. Jesus led the way in fulfilling the law to establish a new order. Conflict was the process. It is for us, now, as well.

Paul Mickey and Robert Wilson have provided leadership toward this end through their book, *Conflict Resolution: Case Study*. Conflict, they maintain, is the birthright of the church.[17] Mickey and Wilson contribute again to the understanding of conflict as a means whereby one moves from chaos and disruptional change toward reconciliation in the church. Conflict therefore becomes an integral part of Christian theology and ministry. They also affirm the dynamics of power negotiation in the church as an important aspect of church growth and reconciliation. Conflict enables us to move beyond apathy, complacency, and feelings of powerlessness, and brings a focus to specific issues that allows us to enter into negotiation and ultimately toward resolution and reconciliation. Chaos, apathy, anger, confusion, doubt may be the beginning point, but the conflict that may be generated as a response can enable us to move toward the possibilities and risks required for reconciliation. This means growth for each of us as well as for our organization.[18]

The most ready areas for conflict in the church are also the very areas where growth is both needed and possible. Acceptance and reconciliation are at the center of such growth in these areas. The following areas have been selected by Mickey and Wilson:

1. Faith differences. Responding to such differences can move along a continuum from open to antagonistic. Handling such differences requires a sensitive awareness of them and assurance that differences do have integrity.

2. Church staff conflicts. Such things as personality clashes, goal differences, personal perceptions of ministerial task and calling, all combine for potential for staff conflict. Some suffering at the point of loss of autonomy for individuals on the staff may be necessary for the achievement of greater goals of the group or of the church. Such will be accomplished only through the help of the supportive, accepting, and reconciling help of the congregation itself.

3. Pastor-parish relations. This area of conflict recognizes the differing concepts of what the church is, in the minds of the various people in the parish. Goals, nature, and purpose of the church can feed into divisiveness or can provide the input for an increase in the understanding of the church by all. At this point, the pastor may be involved either as a participant or a victim. Growth for all comes through the realization of the potential for reconciliation.

4. Local church mergers and relocations. Such changes involve tremendous threat and loss for some people. Security lies in the old environment. Rational arguments do not help, for the emotions of security are involved. Sorrow and grief are vital aspects of this conflict and must be recognized before the possibility for new life can arise. People need acceptance and support to regain and reinvest themselves in new life following the death of an old life. This can neither be rushed nor ignored.

5. Ecumenical conflict. This may not be as frequent as some of these other areas of conflict. It does involve the church where there are more than one denomination in its support as well as the situation of churches of different denominations attempting to work together in some cooperative parish organization. Conflict in this area may also develop between denominational administrators as they attempt to start new congregations in expanding areas.

6. Establishing program goals. This is probably a most common area for conflict to develop, but it also provides great potential for individual and organizational growth through acceptance and reconciliation. The dimensions for concern noted here are in leadership style,

goal selection methods, types of goals, and means of developing priorities.

7. Relating to denominational representatives. Depending on the ecclesiastical structure of the church, a local church can find itself involved in controversy with its executive agency or staff. A major area of conflict here can be the denomination pushing its program down on the local church, competing for time and resources with the local program. Their goals can conflict and distrust can develop. Pastors have a habit of getting caught in the middle of such conflict. Growth will most probably be realized here with a successful combination of both larger denominational and local church programming.[19]

The isolation of these areas and bringing them to our consciousness can be helpful as we look at the role of conflict in church growth and reconciliation. The atmosphere of support and acceptance and the goal of ultimate reconciliation are necessary if these vital areas of church life are to be constructive rather than a destructive conflict of interests.

Reconciliation may be viewed as that security within the church which frees us from having to demand that others agree with our own point of view. Dissenters are not forced out of the fellowship. We can choose to show how Christians can be reconciled to the differing ways that the Holy Spirit works in each individual and group in the church. Our task is to learn to practice this reconciliation within the church, for we must also choose to practice it in the broken and alienated society around us. The mission of the church is reconciliation and healing, and we receive this call from God "who through Christ, reconciled us to Himself and gave us the ministry of reconciliation" (2 Corinthians 5:18). This call to reconciliation leads us to the necessity of recognizing both realism and idealism as part and parcel of local church life. We need also to accept the disunity and tension that result from accepting both of these dynamics and find our way to reconciliation.

John M. Miller leads us to this acceptance in his book, *The Contentious Community*. Miller reminds us that the church must have some idealism. Christ certainly carried an idealistic message and attempted to raise the sights of all those around him. We are also emphatically reminded that the church must have some realism. Understanding the nature of people, including Christians, will help us in this imperative. A balance or tension between both idealism and realism should lead us to a healthy climate for church growth. Miller reminds us that either realism or idealism can slip into cynicism, and when we do become cynical, we fall into a very troublesome trap. Idealists need to give their best strength to the church as well as realists. In fact, most probably both polarities are represented, however minutely, in every person. Cynicism, however, should never be tolerated.[20]

We do need to recognize that the church has grown into an incredibly complex organization. A significant part of that growth has been a wide diversity within. Many avenues are open for persons to find their role and contribution somewhere in its wider ranks. Some of this has been accomplished through the wide range of church denominations. Otherwise, this diversity can be found in factions or subgroups within single denominations and local churches. John Miller suggests that all of us cannot be right. However, we can be accepted because it is God's truth which still abides. It is inevitable that we shall disagree with what that truth is and how it applies to us in our time. But in the end, our diversity with its resultant fighting can be seen not as a fight to the death, but a fight for new life. We fall into troublesome complacency when we cease to debate the questions that may be raised. Church battles can therefore be a sign of life and hope, whereas dullness brings deadness. Miller even reaches for the point that our church battles really reflect the conflict which God feels over what should be done and what the proper direction is for the world and the church.[21] Reconciliation finds many means of expression.

A part of the realism that the church needs to accept for itself is that we humans have the capacity both for hostility toward each other as well as toward God. The repression of such hostility, and possibly the consciousness thereof, creates a tremendous sense of guilt and low self-worth. Our past tends to constitute what we now are, and influences what we do. The recognition of our past hostility is necessary before we become freely reconciled to be new beings with God.

The implication for life in the church follows that we need both acceptance and reconciliation. Where will we find it? Without such recognition of hostility and its acceptance and reconciliation within the church, the life and work of the church becomes superficial. We find ourselves called to love God in worship when we, at the same time, ambivalently hate God and one another. A look through the Psalms will find many an example of this expression of humanity. It becomes important for the ministry of reconciliation of the church to allow this ambivalence to come out, and to find its reconciliation. The church could be the place, and needs to be the place, for this acceptance of hostility. We can accomplish this task if we lessen the defensiveness within the individual to hear the message of the gospel. This is just as true for children in the church as it is for their parents and other adults. Pastoral counseling is a logical place where this acceptance can be experienced and reconciliation begun. However, it also needs to be experienced in such areas as church school and other growth groups which are part of a vital church program.

This calling even reaches into the council or administrative boards. This acceptance of hostility then becomes critical for carrying out a teaching and growth-oriented ministry.[22]

Dynamically, every organization must find reconciliation as the membership of that organization strives for some kind of product which will satisfy its fulfillment. The important aspect of this dynamic is the how factor, or control of how that satisfaction is to be brought about. A win/win methodology necessitates the satisfaction of all, not just partial satisfaction which you can achieve by the use of Robert's Rules of Order, giving the winning group their satisfaction and the losing group a loss of worth and esteem. The acceptance of all, and the satisfaction for all, requires a process which utilizes the conflict, turning its power back into the whole organization such that fulfillment is experienced by all. This can be symbolically shown as follows:

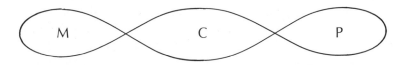

The above symbol indicates the interweaving of the power of conflict to integrate the factors of (M) membership (the who), (C) control (the how), and (P) the product (satisfaction). Such dynamic increases the whole of the organization. Another symbol demonstrates the inadequate utilization of the force of conflict. Only partial satisfaction results from this dynamic. It shows the lack of acceptance and reconciliation which is our main theme and concern at this point.

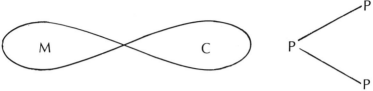

The above symbol shows the neurotic cycle which can be found in the dynamic of dealing with membership, control, and product. Only partial satisfaction is experienced by members and the energy flows back upon itself without an inclusive product of satisfaction for all. This conflict generally produces a scapegoat, often experienced in the church as the dismissal or replacement of the pastor. No solution is found for the whole, only for a portion who came off with a win in the win/lose relationship.[23]

When the church wins the battle within itself in the utilization of conflict through acceptance and reconciliation for church growth, the world outside the church wins also, for it is the whole world that Christ gave as a mission for the church. The church as organization and fellowship needs to become united in order to give its best in the strategy to share the good news for the whole world. This is the winning that matters. One of the ways of getting this message out into the world, using the model of conflict and reconciliation, is the model of community organization. How can the ministry of reconciliation be accomplished through a community organization that often promotes differences in order to dramatize issues? This is a dilemma of the Christian community as it looks to promote social justice in the community around it. Given the command to choose the way of reconciliation, Christians have discovered that they can act with the use of non-violent conflict without degeneration into violence. Conflict and reconciliation are not incompatible as forces turned loose in the community. It remains true that not all conflict is necessary and that we need to minimize unnecessary conflict. The ministry of reconciliation is the inheritance of all, and it becomes a part of the ministry of the church to bring that message to the alienated of society as well as to those receiving satisfaction from that society.

Lyle Schaller shares this concept with the church. He hopes that the primary purpose of community organization will be seen as the helping of individuals to develop and use the resources that God has given them in the control of their own destiny and the destiny of their communities. This empowerment is a part of the ministry of reconciliation as the church mobilizes its own resources to meet such needs in the community around it and of which it is a part. This process must include the dimensions of love, justice, redemption, reconciliation, mercy and judgment of God.[24]

The understanding of the concept of reconciliation and the dynamics it provides in the midst of conflict plays a large part in the utilization of conflict for the growth of the church as an organization, as well as for its individual members.

SELF-ACTUALIZATION

Self-actualization can truly begin after self-acceptance and reconciliation have taken place as developed in the prior sections. We can begin the work of actualizing the self as well as actualizing the organization of which we are a part when conflict is accepted as something that we have created, rather than that which has happened to us. When we come out of the image of the victim into the image of the creator, growth noticeably occurs. Actualization for all in an organization occurs when there is no attempt to avoid disagreements with vague and ambiguous compromises, nor to determine to pull apart because of these basic differences. Instead, all sides must acknowledge the validity of what others are doing and find reconciliation in the common mission, however varied may be the style and tactic. Participation means sharing with both feeling and action, joining together in the work of the Spirit, both in the church and the world. Our experience of community on the road to self-actualization is not just a romantic feeling. We participate in the fellowship of reconciliation, realizable only through the fellowship of suffering. This seems to be the experience of the early Christian community as Paul reports it to us throughout his letters in the New Testament. The suffering servant concept seems to be a key throughout our biblical history on the way toward self-actualization and realization of the church as mission.

Growth and self-actualization for the individual seems to parallel such actualization for the church as well. There will always be a meaningful past that must be recognized for its place in the life of the individual as that person strives further for self-actualization. Appreciation for the past as well as a yearning for a new future are part of the ambivalence as the individual seeks growth. We as individuals both want and do not want change to take place. We like who we are on the one hand, yet are dissatisfied enough to want to be someone we are not yet. The church faces the same dynamics. For many in the church, the past represents a golden age which has considerable meaning for its older members who have trouble adjusting physically or emotionally to radical new demands for change. At the same time, it becomes necessary for those members who resist change to find tolerance and acceptance of those who believe that God is calling them to participation in a changing role for the church. This tests for koinonia. The experience of such crises in the church presents the most dynamic opportunities for growth and self-actualization, while at the same time represents some danger to the stability and cohesiveness of that fellowship. If the tension becomes too threatening, growth can be arrested. Self-actualization will occur when we move from the question of what can we do about those "others" in our fellowship to how can we utilize all our resources together to do the job of the mission to which we are called. As long as we tend to prefer the tried and the true process that we have known, however adequate or inadequate, to the risk of change, we sacrifice the real possibility of self-actualization. Both theologically and psychologically, we are aware that it is through suffering that we grow, and it is through conflict that the church will be actualized. There are no short cuts and no easy ways.

Blundering should not be the only way to go into suffering. It does behoove us to learn the sensitivity to timing. We need not force issues or create situations for the sake of pushing something through in order to have suffering, and therefore actualization. The skill of understanding timing is a part of being at one with the Spirit in the community of the church. Creative leadership intends to keep issues open and fluid within the organization in order that there will be a gradual evolution and change which will maximize the possibility of maintaining the unity of the fellowship with the diversity of opinion throughout. Timing is not always man-made, but often a part of the contribution of the Spirit. I believe the ultimate in understanding self-actualization for the church, and for us as individuals within it, comes from the statement of Jesus, "Whoever would save his life will lose it, and whoever loses his life for my sake will find it" (Matt. 16:25). This is a hard lesson to learn, but the experience of learning it is one of the most exhilarating that we can anticipate.

As Lyle Schaller reminds us from his analysis of the work of social change agents, power and its redistribution is an important part of social actualization. New centers of power may be necessary in order for such actualization to take place. This can be true in both the situation of the church in relationship to the community around it, as well as descriptive of the internal dynamics of the church itself. This redistribution of power can be the rejuvenating force which allows for new growth to take place. The Christian's interest in the goal of change for both self and the organization of the church is not based upon personal aggrandizement or gain, but rather on the goal of helping each person or group realize the full potential of their God-given resources.

Actualization will occur when we choose to get involved and quit merely observing. Such a choice commits our own future into interaction with others who seek their actualization likewise. Commitment to a helping ministry creates the possibilities for actualization for all. To become a Christian is to be changed. Being changed persons, we find that we are led to helping others change and grow as persons in Christ. This is the calling of God, the ministry of helping to provide relationships with others whereby individuals, as well as the whole of a group, find help to change. These helping relationships provide the opportunity for people to open their lives to the guidance of the Holy Spirit. This actualization cannot happen through coercion or force, but must be made by the individual's own response. We can help provide that opportunity by helping to provide the caring, helping relationship.

This opportunity for actualization requires a faith in the potential within each of us both to grow and to help others to grow. It is the understanding in faith that the Holy Spirit is capable of working both in the self and in others, and that each self has unconditional self-worth. Jesus showed us the way by his appreciation of persons as they were at the point of his interaction with them. However, he portrayed the deep-seated belief in the possibility of new life for persons that goes well beyond their present state of achievement. Our involvement in the helping ministry within the community of the church has the potential for us to find our own actualization in the mutual interaction of the fellowship. Being in the helping ministry costs in terms of faith, energy, and time. We can be willing to suffer because we believe in the potentiality within the relationships for the operation of change by the Holy Spirit.

Others, therefore, play a critical role in the realization of self-actualization, both for the self and the larger organization. Each member of the helping community becomes an instrument to the enabling relationship which allows the Holy Spirit to work amongst us all. Each can be renewed by the spirit of relationship with others and God and achieve that actualization which is our God-given potentiality. The conflict which runs through the suffering and reconciliation emerges as growth for self and other.[25]

We turn now to more specific ideas for the educational program in the church through the structuring of conflict.

Notes

1. M. C. Hendrickson, "Conflict in a Future Shocked Church," *Journal of Pastoral Care* 25, no. 2 (1972): 77–81.

2. Harold R. Fray, Jr., *Conflict and Change in the Church* (Boston: Pilgrim Press, 1969), pp. 4–5.

3. Ibid., p. 22–24.

4. Speed Leas and Paul Kittlaus, *Church Fights: Managing Conflict in the Local Church* (Philadelphia: Westminster Press, 1973), pp. 16–17.

5. Ibid., pp. 20–24.

6. Ibid., pp. 35–41.

7. Gerald M. Phillips, Douglas J. Pedersen, and Julian T. Wood, *Group*

Discussion: A Practical Guide to Participation and Leadership (Boston: Houghton-Mifflin Co., 1979), pp. 53–60.

8. Charles A. Dailey, "The Management of Conflict," *Chicago Theological Seminary Register,* ed. Perry D. LeFevre, 59, no. 4 (May 1969): 3.

9. Charles A. Dailey, "Reflections on the Elmhurst Case," *Chicago Theological Seminary Register,* ed. Perry D. LeFevre, 59, no. 4 (May 1969): 11–14.

10. Charles P. Jaeger, ed., *Utilizing Conflict: A Learning System* (Nashville: Discipleship Resources, 1976), pp. 6–7.

11. Rensis Likert and Jane Likert, *New Ways of Managing Conflict* (New York: McGraw-Hill, 1976), pp. 54–55.

12. Ibid., pp. 65–66.

13. Ibid., pp. 66–67.

14. Ibid., p. 73.

15. Ibid., pp. 141–145.

16. Ibid., pp. 157–183.

17. Paul A. Mickey and Robert L. Wilson, *Conflict Resolution: A Case Study Approach to Handling Parish Situations* (Nashville: Abingdon Press, 1973), pp. 14–18.

18. Ibid., pp. 31–33.

19. Ibid., pp. 55–148.

20. John M. Miller, *The Contentious Community* (Philadelphia: Westminster Press, 1978), pp. 27–36.

21. Ibid., pp. 97–99.

22. Gordon Jackson, "The Problem of Hostility: Psychologically and Theologically Considered," *Journal of Religion and Health* 11, no. 1 (1972): 84–93.

23. Credit goes to Blaine F. Hartford of the Niagara Institute of Behavioral Science for this model.

24. Lyle E. Schaller, *Community Organization: Conflict and Reconciliation* (Nashville: Abingdon Press, 1966), pp. 130–138.

25. Jackie Smith, *Leading Groups in Personal Growth* (Richmond, Va.: John Knox Press, 1973), pp. 149–153.

PART II

UTILIZING CREATIVE CONFLICT
TO ENHANCE EDUCATION
IN THE CHURCH:
GENERAL CONSIDERATIONS

7 The Uses of Conflict: Psychological and Educational Considerations

The emphasis now is to shift more specifically to the educational program in the church. Part II will be more on the general considerations, and Part III will be focused upon specific procedures. Having now been presented with a background in the psychological, sociological, and theological dynamics of conflict and their application to church growth, we move more to the uses of conflict as it may enhance education in the church. This particular chapter will deal with the psychological and educational considerations of such use.

Like most other movements, the Christian education movement has been characterized by change. The general field of education as well has been marked by the same dynamics. Where there is change, there is the potential for conflict. The question remains: How is that conflict used, and how will it be used as we go through this flux all about us? Has it been a creative experience, and will it be a creative experience, particularly as we look to education in the church?

There may be some question about the meaning of education when it is referred to in this writing. I prefer not to limit education to an understanding of a program such as the Sunday School program of a church. I see education rather as the experience of the whole church or the total action of the church as a congregation. I would tend to agree with the focus of education which author-teacher James Michael Lee suggests for religious instruction. Our concern here is with Christian living, or the integration of the individual's personality structure and that person's behavior along the lines we can call Christian.[1] I would continue with Lee to focus on the person and the person's experiencing of life, not just learning about life. This experience is a very existential Now, but we also must find ways to integrate the history of religious experience into the personal Now. This is not just an isolated individual's experience; it is important to understand it as a socialization process. Values and attitudes are not learned in isolation, but rather in socialization with like-minded persons. Persons do their learning in community, and in particular in the church as it learns to utilize its asset of the Christian community.[2]

I find it important also to embrace another educational concept which Lee has championed. This theory is referred to as the "structuring theory" for education. This theory suggests that teaching involves a very deliberate and conscious structuring of the learning situation. Lee further defines this structuring as "the various physical, emotional, socially climatological, and product-process elements of a lesson which are so arranged that they tend to effect the desired learning outcomes."[3] Planning for this kind of education is strategic and relates to a goal of modifying behavior. This is a student or learner-centered design which focuses on the process as well as the product.

This reference to educational theory will find elaboration

throughout Part II. It should be obvious that the learner-centeredness will draw us into developmental educational theory with psychological understanding necessary. Given the theory of Part I, it is natural to see that conflict fits very nicely into a learner-centered, process-oriented educational program. We need to pursue the psychological and educational considerations further.

PSYCHOLOGICAL CONSIDERATIONS

The concept of developmental psychology has provided a most helpful foundation for education in the church. It recognizes human development as an on-going process as a result of interaction between a personality and the environment. The shape of the personality comes over the course of the years of development, and the shape takes form as a result of the decisions within interaction. A particular type of developmental psychology that has found a most accepted place in church education is ego psychology. This school indicates that the ego has its own development as a result of its role of playing mediator between the inner development of the self and the self's relationship with the environment. The most influential ego psychologist that has affected church education has been Erik Erikson.

Erikson has developed his psychology in a series of stages in which the ego processes a new sense of itself at each stage. This follows the pattern indicated earlier in Part I of this book about a conflict resolution process. At each stage of the ego's development, the ego must find a successful resolution to the conflict that arises and provide a synthesis of the positive and negative aspects. This provides us with a psychological base for a conflict utilization educational theory.

Erikson says the ego development over a lifetime follows

some form of epigenetic schedule through eight major stages. Each of these stages has within it the necessity of conflict resolution. Internal conflict develops in the person's sense of self, and a resolution is needed in order to move from that stage of psycho-social crisis to the next. A listing of the psycho-social crises for Erikson is as follows:

1. Basic trust versus basic mistrust
2. Autonomy versus shame
3. Initiative versus guilt
4. Industry versus inferiority
5. Identity versus role confusion
6. Intimacy versus isolation
7. Generative versus stagnation
8. Ego integrity versus despair[4]

The particular way in which the person's ego deals with these crises forms the bases for the personality structure of that person.

If we continue to pursue the basic human development theory in psychology, we are led to the work of Jean Piaget and his theory of structuralism. This developmental psychology of Piaget is of assistance to us in education because of the way that it suggests the transformation of the cognitive structures through stages like those of Erikson. There is an increasing complexity of the stages as one continues to interact with the environment. Piaget outlines the structure and capacity of persons in their mental and personality development, which gives us a basic structure of knowledge and how ideas can be structured for persons at different age levels. This has been of particular value in the concern for education that is relevant to the point of development of the individual.[5] Within these structural stages are limits which need to be seriously considered in attempts at education. These stages of Piaget may be described in general terms as follows:

1. The first stage is the sensory-motor intelligence which describes the interaction between the child and the environment through the physical action.
2. The second stage in this developmental theory is that of pre-operational intelligence. This phase is described as the general move from action to mentality. It is a period of great development of the intelligence where partially organized constructs or intuitions are developed.
3. The third phase is that of concrete operations which may be described as a transition to the use of a coherent and integrated cognitive system for organizing the world around the person. There is a structuring that is possible of things in the present in relation to those in the past. The attempt here is for the person to organize all that confronts him/her in the present.
4. The fourth and final stage is that of formal operational intelligence which allows the child to move toward the peak of his/her intellectual maturity in the structural sense. Real strides are made in the developmental process at this point. Oppositional thinking is allowed, and hypothetical solutions can be examined for their consequences.

By a process that may be seen to be similar to Erikson, each phase that the person goes through has a state of equilibrium which faces conflict and breaks down as complexity develops. For instance, there is an important move in the development from pre-operational, where representational thought is learned, to the next stage of concrete operations where there is recognition of simple, logical relationships.

The experience which helps bring this change about is the utilization of the conflict that is faced as the pre-operational period moves toward the potential of the concrete operational. When the person comes up against something which is beyond the structure of the stage of reasoning he/she is in, the experience brings doubt and contradiction into the perception of what is true. This creates disequilibrium. Movement toward restructuring proceeds because of the conflict, however, and leads to the restructuring and recognizing of the possibility of logical relationships. Growth and learning are the direct results of this conflict.

Considerable research in relationship to this psychological theory of development has been done by Lawrence Kohlberg and Ronald Goldman, as well as by James Fowler. These educational developments will be discussed in the following section of this chapter. Such developmental models have formed the foundation for much of the research and progress in educational developments used in our churches. Further psychological developments should be noted before moving on to the educational considerations.

It is well known that Freudian psychology has contributed the concept of the superego which is the suggested locus for the parental and community-based codes of conduct learned in a developmental process of the person. The superego provides an inhibitory process by which we get feedback on what is right and wrong. If we attempt to move against the indicator of the superego, we experience the feeling of guilt. This sets up the conflict between the imposition of values through the superego by parent and community with our own desires and instincts coming out of the id. Again, we are in a conflict situation that must be resolved by the person, and that resolve comes through the development of the ego, as has been suggested earlier. The ego must provide the mediation which allows for the conflict to be resolved. This process may be described as the development of the conscience. Education has found this psychological concept by Freud a helpful image.

The society is also a basic source for the shaping of the moral life of the person. Society organizes and formalizes the values which the individuals bring to it. These create a powerful influence on all those who live together. These values, distilled from individuals' actions and opinions, provide the bases for choice as individuals mature and become more socialized. The values come from the particular group of persons with whom we associate and mature. The family is the basic source, but the wider family of society creates the more comprehensive values.

It may seem that the individual has very little to do with the shaping of his/her own maturity and development. Again, we find the individual in the struggle between the self and the external environment of parents and society. This internal conflict comes from the external influence of a moral code, the internal grappling with it, and then personal assimilation and adaption of it to fit the individual's needs. As individuals, we tend to mature at different rates and with different parts of our individual struggle.

The developmental concepts of psychology reviewed here have as their common point the bringing of the individual into intra-psychic conflict at each of several stages in order to move through the emerging potential of the individual in the maturing process. At each crisis, there is a situation which provides a block to that person's utilization of past experience and understanding. This period is a struggling one as the individual strives to order past learning with present experience and possibility. The ego provides the center for this interaction and is the source for the resultant creative activity which allows for the overcoming of the crisis and the movement toward new understanding with its further elaboration and consolidation. This is conflict utilization described psychologically.

We find this dynamic particularly involving the affective dimension, as well as the cognitive dimension, in the maturing process of youth/adolescence. This personality development time for youth reflects heavy inner conflicts of the affective dimension where dependence/independence is in major conflict. Tension, frustration, and aggression are major emotional feelings as youth attempt to deal creatively with their internal conflict. This affective dynamic of the developmental system needs to be taken much more seriously in our educational processes in the church than we have been willing to for a good part of our history. It is at this stage of youth/adolescence that we find a peak of intrapersonal conflict between the aggressive impulses within the self and its development and the socially sanctioned moral norms of behavior. This refers to our earlier reference in this chapter to the development of the conscience and values.

These psychological considerations have great import as we begin to build our educational theory. Let us turn now to the educational considerations as we attempt to utilize conflict constructively for the growth of persons.

EDUCATIONAL CONSIDERATIONS

Earlier in this chapter, reference was made to the structuring theory proposed by James Michael Lee. This theory builds on the idea that "teaching consists in the deliberate, conscious structuring of a learning situation so that the desired learning outcomes are effected."[6] It is important that this structuring be a conscious endeavor in which the student is led very openly to specified and desirable learning outcomes. We seek after the experience that overcomes the usual second-hand experiencing of religious knowledge. Education in this system is quite complex, planned, and finds inter-relationships the basis of the learning experiences. It is more difficult than the mere transmission of information from one head to another. We are after not only the cognitive skill, but the emotional maturity which is the affective development in the growth of the student in religious education.

It is important to plan for two results in this structuring theory. Lee makes it clear that we must expect subject products as well as the cognitive, affective, volitional, physical, and religious processes.[7] This product is referred to as a particularized, static, and usually tangible content. Process refers more to the generalized but more dynamic intangible content.[8] It is intended that the product is important, but if the product is achieved without an understanding of the process, then there is an incompleteness to the education, possibly interfering with retention. The process must be learned in order to discover how to achieve the right product again and again. It is most important to allow for the attitude to change to show the developing, growing change that is going on in the individual as he/she comes to learn a product. Here we are finding a combination of the cognitive and the affective in the learning situation. If the cognitive is the goal without the achieving of the affective, then we have left out much of what we call religious. Structuring can definitely help us achieve both products.

A vital dimension to the inclusion of the affective and the cognitive is the dimension of the non-verbal in the teaching process. If we take seriously the move from the teacher or teacher-centered to the student-centered format for the classroom, we will find that the move toward non-verbal experience is natural and provides a goodly portion of the teaching methodology and material. We move into a significant area of education when we match this non-verbal with the verbalization of the experience that was had in the classroom, allowing the student to learn expression of the feeling that he or she has discovered in the structured experience. Experiences need reflection as well as expression, and the teacher's sensitivity to the student's difficulties of getting in touch with the meaning of the experience in the classroom will help greatly that student's subject product as well as the understanding of the process.

Conflict is often experienced in the classroom in the dimension of control versus freedom. Both at home and in the classroom, the younger student is particularly aware of who is in control. In our earlier theoretical discussion of conflict, it was made clear that the degree to which there was a felt imbalance in the equilibrium of power made the person become either competitive or collaborative. Where power equilibrium was felt, the tendency was toward collaboration. There is much more of a feeling of openness and receptivity when there is a combination of teacher control and student control in the classroom. The feeling tone, or the social climate, in the classroom becomes a very important dimension for structuring education. The social climate is important as one attempts to deal with attitude formation in the student. This is particularly true as we look at affective education and less true in the concerns for cognitive effect. The equilibrium, or social climate of the classroom, will have much to do with the success of the learning of a process in structured education in the classroom for religious education.

As we learned in the psychological considerations, when we attempt to structure experiences it is important that we understand the structures and capacities of the persons whom we wish to teach. Their mental and personality development must be understood as one plans for the teaching of some core ideas at different age levels. Not all things are possible for all people at the different ages or stages of growth. Church education cannot ignore this as a plan for, or structure of, religious experiences.

Robert L. Browning takes notice of this fact as he advocates a systems approach to church education. He sees it important in the whole of church-wide education that the systems which exist in the church be brought together in a working order to achieve common objectives. Each of the sub-systems in the church must function with their standards in order for the objectives of the whole church to be reached, especially those of education.[9]

Browning has listed the key systems and sub-systems of the church in his summary listing. He lists the following seven key elements:

1. The structure and quality of the development of the person in the stages of mental and personality development
2. The structure and quality of the core ideas and experiences within the Christian faith which guide objectives and ground the education biblically, theologically, and historically
3. The structure and quality of the learning environment which describes the inter-relationship between teachers, learners, resources, facilities, and methods in order that the Christian faith can be appropriated in their lives
4. The structure and quality of local church education planning which brings together persons, resources, training designs, and evaluation procedures with the management systems for the local church

5. The structure and quality of general church curricular and program resources which relates to the development of curricular materials, leadership patterns to bring together clear objectives
6. The structure and quality of the church (local to international), which is the way the church speaks to its objectives in the community and the world
7. The structure and quality of overall society, which is the source of the values which come to us[10]

Browning feels that the fourth sub-system so listed is crucial because it is the local church management system. These planners keep the first three systems inter-related and functioning. It seems to me that the sixth sub-system is one which is also critical, for in it Browning feels that this is where the values learned in the classroom are related to what is happening in the whole life of the church. We are aware that education takes place all the time and the informal is of as much import as the formal, while we consider values and attitudes of what a Christian is and does. It is at this point that I would hope that integration takes place and that the education that goes on in religious instruction is seen as one. The total education of the church takes place in the living out of the Christian community. In a systems approach, all systems must reinforce one another for effectiveness.

INTEGRATION—THE MOVEMENT FROM DISEQUILIBRIUM TO EQUILIBRIUM

It is at this point of integration that we come into relationship with Piaget's concept of structuring for education. Looking at the child's mind, Piaget's research has shown us that the mind develops structures which are actively transforming and restructuring the experiences which are coming in from the world around the child. It is an organization of the experience that is the important component as we look at education and change. The primary source of motivation for the child in the learning process is to get to a state of equilibrium from disequilibrium. When the child is out of equilibrium, or in disequilibrium, the motivation is to learn what will bring equilibrium again. New structures are formed in this accommodation process, and learning is assimilated. The child or individual moves from states of disequilibrium to equilibrium and back and forth, facing new problems and experiences, finding new needs, and discovering new techniques of controlling and growing from the world around. The individual way in which this takes place is what leads us to our own individual differences.[11] It is the utilization of the conflict that the individual faces in moving from disequilibrium to equilibrium that is the creative aspect of the educational process. Growth occurs as the new problems are faced, the conflicts diagnosed, and the new experiences integrated into the movement from one stage of growth to the next. If this is not accomplished, disintegration, deterioration, and arrested development are apt to occur.

If we take the developmental concept of Piaget and others seriously, we are led to the necessity of looking to methods for learning which can be individualized to relate to where the learner is in his/her growth pattern. Browning feels that religious education has come to learn some of this and to utilize learning by doing. However, he feels that oftentimes this is not oriented to the very core ideas or the basic relationships of the Christian faith. If learning by doing is utilized in relation to core ideas, it is further important that persons learn to reflect on the meaning of that activity and discovery and find ways to order this information and experience in accordance with its meaning for them individually. It is at this point that we often break down in our educational process. Our teachers are not able to help the integration process after they have been able to bring into activity some of the ideas and objectives which they have for their educational plan.

The emphasis for religious education in this systems approach comes down to three imperatives:

1. The need to be more conscious of and define core ideas, basic understandings, and relationships, which are fundamental to the Christian life
2. The discerning of the consistent understandings, facts, ideas, and attitudes which are most appropriate for the child at the various age levels
3. These co-ideas and attitudes must then be put into a series of learning experiences appropriate to the structures of the learner's mind and to the personal affective life with those around him/her[12]

Lest there be the feeling that there is too much emphasis upon individualization, I would affirm the need for balance between that and the group experience. It has been made clear that we cannot forget individual differences as well as general stages for growth and development of age levels. However, we must continue to remember that much can be taught by the community and through the community, and that considerable learning is involved by bringing persons together into meaningful relationships. It is therefore a combination of individual and group process which will help the person through the appropriate tasks for learning, both mentally and emotionally, in religious education. When we learn how to evaluate what we do, we will have better strategies for on-going learning than is the usual experience of education in the church. We can only evaluate when we have been able to set clear objectives, understand the processes we are using to achieve those objectives, and have a method of evaluation; we can then say whether we have, in fact, achieved or not achieved the goals and objectives of our educational planning. Structuring should help us, if we structure intentionally and with a knowledge of cognitive and affective material. It is through structuring that we will be able to program the use of conflict to utilize it maximally to help a person move through the various stage levels that we have discovered in our developmental educational theories, finding new equilibrium along the way.

It is this attempt to blend the combined values of individual education and the individual in relation to the Christian community that draws a person together in ego morality. C. Ellis Nelson helps us understand this relationship in his work "Conscience, Values, and Religious Education."[13] Education is seen as more than just what happens in a classroom. The dynamic between the individual and the community of believers becomes the open classroom. The congregation, then, becomes a major area for the development of ego morality. It is in the work and worship of the congregation that the person finds an example of moral standards in his/her forming and re-forming. This is discovered both in the larger congregation as well as subgroupings within the congregation. A subgrouping such as the boards and committees of the church is an integral part of where an individual displays the true values and attitudes that are both individually affirmed and corporately affirmed. Younger persons have a way of seeing what adults do in these subgroupings and therefore discovering the true values that are expressed in the community.

Another area of development in religious education that is

useful here is the methodology called "values clarification."
It is somewhat revealing to have both children and adults
experience the clarification process. Conflict can be positively used as the values clarification process brings one face
to face with the realities of his/her valuing and attitudes. From
that point, one can decide whether one wants to affirm what
has been clarified or work toward the establishment of new
priorities in the conscience and value life. The support of and
work with the Christian community becomes an important
part of both the clarifying and the re-establishing of new values as new integration comes about.

SIMULATION AS A TOOL FOR VALUES EDUCATION

There is an educational process which can be most helpful
in the establishing of values and the bringing of experiences
into consciousness for new learning and new equilibrium.
This is called simulation and gaming. Simulation has been
defined as a "condensed representation of reality, a simplified
model of a real world system."[14] The simulation is a system
which provides the opportunity to work through life-like
dynamics for learning purposes. It may be done with com-
puter to simulate the system, or it can be done without com-
puter.

A game is more of a contest between players in which there
are established rules and goals or objectives. In the game,
there is a winner that is decided. Games have been used to
create fun with children in the learning process, as well as to
allow them to experience life in a structured way. The game
can be followed by a debriefing of the kinds of roles and rules
that the participants experienced in the game. It is like a
practice for life in which that practice can be replayed or
evaluated without much loss.

Simulation and gaming are combined in education as a way of experiencing life-like learning. The structuring theory described earlier can use simulation games very effectively in setting forth experiences for objectives in the learning schema. It is possible to combine the cognitive learning with the affective learning through this gaming experience.

Conflict can be an integral part of simulation games, and the value of the gaming process is that it can be controlled and utilized by an effective leader, to be followed up with reflection on the conflict that has been experienced. Some very deep feelings can be experienced in this type of education. It therefore needs to have controls put upon it.

Gaming, or exercises for the structure of specific learning, has a way of focusing in on very specific objectives and allowing those objectives to be assessed and integrated in a series leading to larger goals. Some criticism has been made of gaming in that it appears to be manipulative. Sensitive leadership, along with sensitive reflection and debriefing, can overcome any of the dangers that might be encountered in simulation gaming. This type of education is certainly exciting and has a way of motivating students to learn objectives, as well as learn how to learn.

Simulation gaming is a technology that has been able to bridge the problem of moving from the teacher-oriented dispensation of theory to the experience of the learner as he/she actually tries out the theory. Misunderstandings can be overcome, inconsistencies between word and action decrease, and new understanding can come in relatively brief periods of time. It is a safe experience for the most part. It provides the opportunity to try out new experience and new action in an atmosphere which is going to be ultimately supportive and reflective for the good of all. It places conflict in a manageable situation and allows the experience of conflict to be one in both competitive and collaborative experience. The team approach is used as well as the individual approach in such gaming.

As we look to education in the future, some feel that educational simulation games have much to offer the educational planner. Games can help one deal with the fact that change will be a constant. Our lifestyles will constantly be looking toward adaption and problem solving. There will be opportunities for the practice of experimental lifestyle as well as critical problem solving in the future. People will have to learn how to grow and change in shorter periods of time. People will need various skills for problem solving such as the development of the diagnostic and analytic skills which are a valuable product of simulation gaming.[15] Examples of these games will be described in Part III.

The relationship here with the theme of conflict is that in the gaming exercises there is usually a limited supply of resources which are seen as valued. Conflict then can be experienced between teams or between individuals in competition for the resources. Rules help this process be manageable and be a part of a learning rather than a chaotic experience. Values are tested through the conflict. Reflection on the outcome can be most helpful to a person as he/she struggles through the growth stages, moving in and out of equilibrium. Conflict is controllable and can be both competitive and collaborative. The comparison of both competition and collaboration can be made by the individual after having experienced both of them in striving toward goals which are valued. Reflection becomes an important part for the teacher who has structured conflict for educational use. Participants in gaming need time to identify their learnings and to generalize and integrate them into their life experience. Affective as well as cognitive learning comes out of this. The simple or serious identification of feelings, the sharing of them, and the discovery that they are O.K. are important parts of the game debriefing. If the teacher is well prepared for religious education, theological reflection becomes a natural outgrowth of these sharing periods. Meaning comes out of what appears to have been mere play. The excitement of this kind of activity makes learning an experience which will long be remembered rather than shortly forgotten.

THE INTERPRETIVE PROCESS

Another educational consideration needs to be shared in our understanding of the uses of conflict for educational purposes. The interpretive process orders and brings meaning to all of life. It is known best under the "hermeneutical" approach to biblical study, but it has its application to the whole of education and particularly the education that we experience in the church. Hermeneutics describes the interpretive process. Hermeneutics gets into philosophy, language, epistomology, and psychology. It focuses upon the interpreter and the text or object of study.

Biblical studies often become a content process whereby the content of the Bible is "learned" by the student. The teacher supposedly teaches the content of the Bible to the student. The hermeneutical approach focuses upon the student's interpretation of the text. However, both the teacher and the student discover that they have understandings of the text which often differ. How does this become education?

H. Edward Everding, Jr., of The Iliff School of Theology, has outlined the interpretive process as one affecting the whole of our education in the church. Everding indicates that not just the biblical text, but all of life, is interpretation. The general interpretive experience characterizes our life existence. Life then becomes a continuous process of interpretation.[16] To understand how this process works, we must recognize the three basic ingredients:

1. It is important to understand the individual interpreter's own presuppositions. The person, or interpreter, must bring to consciousness and acknowledge his interpretive stance. The interpreter's own preunderstanding has a way of shaping the meaning that will be discovered. Hopefully, this will be a dialogical process, not a monological one.
2. The source to be interpreted is important to recognize. There is distinctiveness in each source, and this may require different questions and skills. Each text or subject may be unique and require analysis and a recognition of intention.
3. The recognition of the difference between the interpreter and the text and an understanding of the distance between the two is critical to be maintained. Interpretation calls for a system which can account for the uniqueness of the text and the interpreter's subjectivity and involvement with that text. One should not confuse this approach with the mastery of a text as subject matter. The text or subject which addresses the interpreter has its value as it calls that interpreter to a decision about his or her own meaning of existence.[17]

The dynamics we have been describing here require understanding of the subject matter of the interpretive process, the understanding of the person, and an understanding of an instructional model. These have been integrated by H. Edward Everding, Jr., Clarence H. Snelling, Jr., and Mary M. Wilcox in a paper entitled "Toward a Theory of Instruction for Religious

Education." (The paper was given at the meeting of the Association of Professors and Researchers in Religious Education, Washington, D.C., November 1976.)

The dynamics of conflict find their way into this hermeneutical approach for learning for life. The first experience of conflict seems to be that moment when the instructor and the student together learn that they are individual or unique interpreters, and that the conflict can come by recognizing that interpretations do vary between individuals because of their own presuppositions which are brought to the process. This naturally forces the direction of learning to that of self-understanding. Why is it that our individual interpretations are so different? Is there merely the content to be learned, or is there more to be learned as the individual confronts a text or subject and learns about himself or herself in relation to it? The inter-relation between heritage and self describes the learning process. Conflict can then be intrapersonal as the individual struggles with polarities within himself/herself, as well as interpersonal as the individual interpretation conflicts with another's interpretation about life and life's experience and meaning. If there can be meaning that comes from the dialogue between individual and text or subject, then that meaning will lead to new self-understandings and to the continuous building up of what we know of as our individual faith.

An important dimension of the Everding/Snelling/Wilcox study is that they relate this interpretation process to an understanding of the developmental nature of the person. We have already reviewed the developmental concepts of Erikson and Piaget, and they review the relationship of these concepts to such theories as those of Lawrence Kohlberg and James Fowler. Each has a way of showing the stages of development within the person.

Lawrence Kohlberg has designed a paradigm for moral reasoning which is set in the six stages of development. These stages of development indicate the need for conflict in order to move between stages. Kohlberg's stages are summarized as follows:

Stage 1—Obedience and Punishment Orientation
This describes the conflict between the ego in its early development and the authority of those in parental or other positions which show superior power.
Stage 2—Naively Egoistic Orientation
This reflects the need to do the right action that will satisfy the self's needs as well as those of others.
Stage 3—The Good Boy Orientation
This describes the inner need to please as well as help others.
Stage 4—Authority and Social Order Orientation
This describes the orientation of doing one's duty and respecting authority for its own sake.
Stage 5—The Contractual Orientation
This is a recognition of the need to have rules in order to maintain individual rights and avoid the violation of others' rights.
Stage 6—Conscience or Principle Orientation
The conscience becomes a directing agent leading to mutual respect and trust.[18]

As in Piaget's and Erikson's developmental model, conflict is experienced as one moves from one stage to another, as well as within stages. Disequilibrium is experienced and resisted, therefore each person needs to bring into equilibrium and order their developmental growth. Conflict of new data requiring personal reorientation is descriptive of the process of education under the developmental model.

This educational design is picked up further by James Fowler as he works out a faith developmental model. He takes six stages and shows how movement follows from the simple to the more complex structures of reasoning in relationship to the faithing process. We can find conflict again working throughout this developmental mode. The Fowler stages are described as follows:

Stage 1—The Intuitive/Projective Stage
   The child or person is imitative and is influenced by the example of others.
Stage 2—The Mythic/Literal Stage
   The person takes a literal approach to appropriating beliefs and moral rules. The authority figures again provide the lead.
Stage 3—The Synthetic/Conventional Stage
   The person places consensus in an important role to find personal meaning. Consensus among peers is primary and becomes the social convention.
Stage 4—The Individuating/Reflexive Stage
   The adolescent becoming adult takes on some responsibility for his or her own lifestyle and attitudes. This stage in particular reflects the dynamic of conflict. Polar tensions are established which put the individual up against the belonging to a community. The self is placed opposite to others and what was once an easy affirmation of consensus becomes now the need to set an image of the self as over against others in self-awareness and responsibility for individual choice.
Stage 5—The Paradoxical/Consolidative Stage
   The person's new self-awareness comes face to face with the need to recognize the integrity of others, contrary to his or her own.

Stage 6—Universalizing Faith
A rare process described as a "Kingdom of God" experience for the person.[19]

Again we are reminded of the need for educational theory to take seriously this structuring of the content and experiences of religious education appropriate to stages of faith as well as moral development of the learner. Conflict should be noted as playing a role in the movement of a person from his/her present stage of development to a new stage.

The instructional model with which Everding, Snelling, and Wilcox conclude is called the confluent process model. As in the interpretive process described earlier, the curriculum in this model holds in tension the emphasis on the text or subject and on the learner. Listening and appropriation become the movement for education. It is similar to Piaget's concept of the twin elements of assimilation and accommodation. An important balance is called for in this confluent model which allows the assimilation/accommodation to move toward equilibrium. This is a holistic approach which joins the processes of the left side and the right side of the brain, a confluence between the cognitive and the affective human responses. Their theory of instruction, therefore, combines the three major processes: 1) the interpreter process, 2) the developmental process, and 3) the confluent process. Each of these processes has within it an important function of conflict to be integrated as a constructive part of the whole educational design.

Within this model, the teacher becomes the change agent. The structuring for learning must take into account the developmental concepts here described and provide for new opportunities for alteration of personal images and structured actions which will allow experimentation to take on new self-awareness and new self-understanding.

This work by Everding, Snelling, and Wilcox from The Iliff School of Theology provides a complex and yet exciting dimension for the strategizing for religious education in times of change such as these in which we are now living.

Educational considerations to this point have been highly individual, taking most seriously the structuring of education according to individual needs, goals, and objectives. The developmental theory of the individual has been posited as a basis for this individual structuring. There are other educational considerations which can have a vital effect on education in the church and which also exemplify the place of conflict in the educational process.

AN ORGANIZATIONAL FOCUS

There are those who maintain that church education is rather an organizational phenomenon. Organizational variables and the climate of such elements as the congregation become the important factors. Church education is affected by its environment, or the context of the congregation. So says Robert C. Worley in his evaluation of church education as an organizational phenomenon. He says the environment and climate of the congregation is as important as what we have been seeing as the structuring of the classroom. For Worley, the local congregation should be the focus of concern in Christian education. What we know of as church education is but one goal task amongst several in any congregation. He lists several conditions in the church organization which make possible effective church education.

1. A precondition for effective church education is that of an achievement-oriented climate. Our preoccupation with the classroom, with curricula and teaching

methods and training, has diverted us from the church organization which must accomplish education's goal.

2. A loss of effectiveness follows power-oriented climates in which the resources and directions of congregational life are drained by energies, persons, money, and other resources. A win/lose situation is fought within the congregation; this generally emanates in a lose/lose situation which is a loss of effectiveness in all areas of the congregation.

3. There is little evidence that congregations which focus on the affiliation-orientation have any real congregational effectiveness. They tend to feel good about each other, but have trouble finding any progress toward goals and objectives.

4. The goalless climate in a congregation, described by an aimlessness, a low level of energy and confusion, is another congregational climate which detracts from any educational goals or objectives. No area again is seen as effective and the prevailing mood is a depression of the spirit.[20]

With these four summations of congregational climates, Worley indicates that interest in teacher training and curricular designs is irrelevant to education. The climate of the congregation destroys any effectiveness therein. His conclusion is that it is the congregation as an entity which does the educating and it is the climate that has the most powerful influence on the goals and tasks of the organization. Our eye should be on the total organizational behavior rather than on the more select image of church education behavior, if we wish to assess the task and evaluation of our educational program.

The congregational climates suggested here have within them the dynamic of conflict in operation. The achievement-oriented style has within it an institutionalization of conflict which allows for the coping mechanisms necessary to direct energies toward goals and objectives. The collaborative approach gives strength to the goals of education in the congregation. In the power-oriented climate, the competitiveness drains off of effectiveness with a loss of energy given to the battle itself. Where there is no conflict, in the goalless congregation, the dynamic influence of conflict is lost. There is no excitement and there is no sharpness that conflict can provide when it is utilized in its positive, constructive dimension. Those congregations which were affiliation-oriented have probably downplayed conflict to the degree that they end up with the concept described earlier as group-think. They felt good about each other, but never allowed the creativity that was within the congregation to emerge because of a fear that it would influence or bring loss of the community and fellowship which they so needed. The congregation is a truly vital entity as we look to the educational goals of the church and the role which conflict can play, either constructively or destructively.

Harold Fray picks up this theme of Worley when he indicates that it is what the church does that is the curriculum of its educational program. The closing of the gap between word and deed is what is necessary if one is to have an effective educational program in the church. Persons must be involved through the decision-making process, rather than having a barrage of words and no experience of the difficulties of making decisions in the neighborhood in which they live. It is the dynamic of being involved in the conflict and controversy within the church that produces the truly educated churchperson.[21]

When persons are involved in the decision-making process of the church, education is going on in the best of classrooms.

When persons are involved in the search for ideas and directions, for clarification and agreement, they are bound to encounter conflict. Conflict tends to polarize attitudes and dispute decision-making proposals, but where trust has been developed and common goals established, there emerges the creative decision making which leads to common agreement on tasks and movement toward consensus. Both individual and group reinforcement can result, which builds the climate of consensus making and creative decision making.

Educational concerns are organizational concerns and organizational concerns do include the individual and his or her striving for meaning. Education occurs in every group interaction and personal interaction in the church congregation as well as in the classroom so structured. We will pursue these various means in the following chapters of this section.

The next chapter will consider further the educational use of conflict as an intentional part of the structuring of educational experiences.

Notes

1. James Michael Lee, *The Shape of Religious Instruction* (Mishawaka, Ind.: Religious Education Press, 1971), pp. 10–42.

2. Ibid.

3. James Michael Lee, "The Teaching of Religion," in *Toward a Future for Religious Education,* ed. J. M. Lee and P. C. Rooney (Dayton, Ohio: Pflaum Press, 1970), p. 59.

4. Erik Erikson, *Insight and Responsibility* (New York: W. W. Norton Co., 1964).

5. Jean Piaget, *The Science of Education and the Psychology of the Child* (New York: Orion Press, 1970).

6. Lee, "The Teaching of Religion," p. 59.

7. Ibid., p. 68.

8. Ibid., p. 76.

9. Robert L. Browning, "The Structure and Quality of Church Education

in the Future," in *Foundations for Christian Education in an Era of Change,* ed. Marvin J. Taylor (Nashville: Abingdon Press, 1976), pp. 138–139.

10. Ibid., pp. 139–140.

11. Ibid., pp. 142–143.

12. Ibid., p. 146.

13. C. Ellis Nelson, "Conscience, Values, and Religious Education," in *Foundations for Christian Education in an Era of Change,* ed. Marvin J. Taylor, pp. 76–77.

14. Paul M. Dietterich, "Simulation-Games Theory and Practice in Religious Education," in *Foundations for Christian Education in an Era of Change,* ed. Marvin J. Taylor, p. 152.

15. Ibid., pp. 160–161.

16. H. Edward Everding, Jr., "A Hermeneutical Approach to Educational Theory," in *Foundations for Christian Education in an Era of Change,* ed. Marvin J. Taylor, p. 42.

17. Ibid., pp. 42–48.

18. Lawrence Kohlberg, "Education, Moral Development and Faith," *Journal of Moral Education* 4 (1974): 5–16.

19. James W. Fowler, "Stages in Faith" (Unpublished paper presented at a symposium at Fordham University, Spring 1975).

20. Robert C. Worley, "Church Education as an Organizational Phenomenon," in *Foundations for Christian Education in an Era of Change,* ed. Marvin J. Taylor, pp. 117–126.

21. Harold R. Fray, Jr., *Conflict and Change in the Church* (Boston: Pilgrim Press, 1969), pp. 29–32.

8 Instructional Conflict: The Planned, Purposive, Deliberative, Goal-Directed Structuring of Conflict

Anyone interested in creative education must consider the value of conflict in the educational process. If, as we have indicated earlier, learning is change, the conflict is the condition for learning. Learning can be defined in terms of some kind of change that is understood at least as the acquisition of new knowledge or new skills. Beyond that, learning involves a change of attitude for a new way of organizing experience and developing commitment to a changed scale of values. The most significant of these changes are those that challenge a person to rearrange the basic commitments around which the person builds a life. This is what we are about when we consider religious education. It draws together the cognitive and affective dimensions of our learning potential and takes place within the accepting love of the Christian community. It is in this context that I wish to set planned, purposive, instructional conflict.

In an earlier reference in the last chapter, the structuring theory of learning was referred to in the work of James

Michael Lee. In this theory, the work of religious instruction turns to that of being a change agent. The agent structures specific experiences leading to specific behaviors which affect the overall Christian lifestyle of the learner. This is accomplished basically through the appropriate structuring of the learning situation in order to modify the behavior of the learner. The educator attempts to operationalize a concept into an experience and to identify specific performances from which religious learning can be developed. Religious instruction, then, becomes the structuring of the learning situation such that the learner's behavior will be modified along the desired religious lines in a fruitful and effective manner.[1]

As I suggested at the beginning of this chapter, this structured learning situation is not just a gathering of isolated individuals. It is a mini-society, or a community influenced by the values of the Christian community. For its true effectiveness, this learning must take place within a fellowship of support, love, and acceptance. Structured learning does have a very specific task or goal, and it must take place within such a community. The community becomes both a context and an object in the learning process. The classroom for religious instruction becomes a life learning lab in which primary experience is the core. It is the learner's interaction with new data and the interaction with the shaped environment which lead to desired changes. As we also learned earlier, it is not just the environment of the classroom about which we speak, but it is the environment of the whole of the church, its activity and congregation, which provides the bases for religious education. Much of what I will be developing in this chapter will have to do with the classroom, but there will be some application to the context as the larger environment of the church.

A simple but beautiful example of structuring conflict into

the classroom by way of shaping the environment was given by James Michael Lee. He tells of a lesson to a third grade class on brotherhood. The teacher set the class into two parts in her planning. The first plart was planned as relatively routine and dull in order to make more sharp the change in the environment, both physical and psychological, for the new learning. After the routine first part, the teacher announced that she had an exciting story to tell to them but that they would need to move to another classroom for that story. There was considerable excitement because of the change, and the children and teacher moved into the neighboring classroom. The children did not know at first that the tables and chairs in that classroom were much heavier than those in the previous room and required more than one to lift a chair or table. The teacher established herself in one corner of the room and asked the children to gather by bringing their chairs and tables closer to her. The conflict was that no individual child could pick up a chair alone and carry it over to the story corner. The weight was too great. She tried to hurry the children to gather together for the story. With some frustration the children tried to pick up a chair and move it to her. With a few leaders diagnosing the problem and teaming up to help one another move the tables and chairs, others soon followed. With cooperation they all gathered together into the story corner. When all were together, the teacher told them their story. The story was also about mutual cooperation and brotherhood. The learning was both verbal and non-verbal and had to occur through the conflict and frustration of moving the tables and chairs.[2] In this type of teaching/learning, both content and attitude formation are products. The structuring process attempts to effect a continuous developing, growing, and changing which lead the individual in community through a transformation of attitudes, values, and beliefs. Both verbal and non-verbal material are integrated into this process.

The purposive, goal-directed structuring of conflict for educational experiences has been given direction and assistance by the work of Robert L. Conrad in a paper called "Creative Learning in Christian Education: The Model of Creative Conflict."[3] In his paper, Conrad analyzed Luther's religious experience and theology and correlated it with the social psychology of creative thought by Arthur Koestler. The creative intrapsychic conflict of Luther's struggle with God is used as a model. The conflict involves 1) conscious conflict, 2) giving up on solving the conflict, 3) sudden insight, 4) interpretation of the new insight.[4] Luther's intrapsychic conflict must be understood for this model.

It was Martin Luther's experience that the Scholastic theology which he had been taught did not jibe with his experience and growing biblical studies. The conflict within him was over the emphasis in Scholastic theology on the ability of persons to utilize their own free will to move toward God and avoid sin. That was the way toward the saving grace given by Christ. On the one hand, a person contributed to the cause of election to salvation by the process just described, and yet Luther had learned from Augustine that persons were justified by grace, not by works. The difficulty for Luther was the discovery of a gracious God in the midst of his attempts to use his own free will to refrain from sin. Luther was caught between an affirmation of the predestination by which God elected him to salvation and, on the other hand, his strong sense of unworthiness of this grace of God. Luther desired grace, but experienced judgment. Conrad analyzes the steps of Luther's struggle in the following way:

1. The active struggle as Luther confronted his two opposing points of view.
2. Luther's experience of passive resignation in contrast to the struggle of the first step.
3. The experience of an unexpected insight toward a resolution of the conflict. A new understanding evolved of the righteousness as a gift of God to humanity, not a demand of God upon humanity. The resolution was a gift receiving faith that provides the right relationship to God without the conflict of the work toward righteousness or justification.
4. The long-range interpretation and integration of the insight that had occurred.[5]

The dynamic of this conflict of Luther is described in the four stages of Koestler's "Creative Act." The stages of this creative process are as experienced by the Luther conflict.

1. A blocked situation which is the conflict
2. A period of incubation
3. The creative act itself
4. The stage of verification, elaboration, and consolidation[6]

Conrad has developed a correlation model between Luther's experience and Koestler's creative act analysis. This correlation moves toward a creative conflict model for teaching and learning. The model involves the four steps which have just been indicated: active struggle, passive resignation, unexpected insight, and long-range interpretation. This model for teaching involves a very specific plan for the structuring of conflict into the lives of the learners. I would like to leave the more specific dimensions of carrying out this conflict model to Part III of this book in which specific procedures will be our concern. The general considerations of such a model are my concern in this chapter.

There is another model which I wish to present that involves the structured use of conflict in the educational process. This model is based on a discussion and decision-making arena. It is based upon a four-phased concept of group interaction which has been presented by B. Aubrey Fisher. The four phases are as follows:

1. Orientation—The searching for ideas and direction in the group with some clarification and agreement in general.
2. Conflict—The beginning of polarization of attitudes, disputing decision-making proposals.
3. Emergence—The beginning to come together in common agreement on task with movement toward consensus.
4. Reinforcement—The emergence of consensus, agreement, and reinforcement of attitudes.[7]

Thomas Scheidel and Laura Crowell have taken these four phases and developed a dynamic concept of two stages as diverging and converging. The first two stages of Fisher above (Orientation and Conflict) are described as a diverging phase which is similar to exploration, examination, and testing. The latter two stages above (Emergence and Reinforcement) are described as converging, or moving through the dynamics of comparison of ideas, evaluation, and finally choice. The two phases, diverging and converging, are like the general dynamic of examination and choosing. At the beginning, individuals feel that they are separate and spar with one another, seeing differences in each other and becoming more defensive. It is like a diverging as individuals and converging to work as a team. The diverging and converging terms are used to separate the process for understanding. The diverging phase emphasizes the creative thinking. The converging phase emphasizes the choice making. Conflict comes into play at the point between the two phases. Conflict is fostered only after the creative, open thinking time has been encouraged. It is important in this first phase to allow for openness to speculation with half-formed ideas which typifies a wide open searching and encouragement of ideas from everyone present. The group or individual must show genuine appreciation of differences of ideas and views and a conscious holding back of evaluation during this phase. The hostility and conflict, then, come at the juncture between diverging and converging, or individual and team. Conflict is encouraged as the desire to move judgment and evaluation. It is a time of narrowing selection and consolidation and shaping ideas of the earlier stage or phase. The moving together as a team creates the rubbing together of ideas leading to the conflict. One taps the positive value of conflict as the movement is toward evaluation and decision making on the part of the whole.[8] Conflict becomes the critical watershed between the diverging and converging phases in this dynamic for learning in groups. More specific procedures will be outlined with this technique in Part III of this book.

Another model suggested earlier by the authors Everding, Snelling, and Wilcox shows a place for the intentional, goal-directed structuring of conflict for education. Their model, based upon developmental concepts of Jean Piaget, suggests an instructional model for religious education that should allow for consolidation of a present or current stage of faith development in the individual, and yet should also be open to the possibility of inducing conflict and enhancing the progress from one stage to another. This is particularly true for the children and youth age groups, but is also applicable to adults in their transition. Attention needs to be paid to the confluent process that brings together both the cognitive and the affective areas for the individual. The structuring takes place by the asking of pointed questions to push for some conflict with present phase development or the staging of an exercise which would bring the individual into conflict to begin the movement toward an advanced stage. It is helpful for the instructor to have a developmental/interpretive grid for the developmental level of the learners. This helps greatly in planning, particularly as one looks to the deliberative structuring of conflict into the educational plan. The instructor takes the role of a change agent. The primal or rooted images which have been established in the learner can then be focused upon, and strategy worked out for enhancing image change. All of this takes place within the context of a learning community for the facilitation of this strategy for image change. Structuring conflict is a deliberative function which leads the learner toward the final act of some action or decision. Reflection and consolidation, then, are necessary as the individual struggles for further self-awareness and self-understanding.[9]

The age level of adolescents or youth is a particularly receptive time to work with education by way of planned, deliberative conflict. Affective relations of youth are especially high, and they seem to respond more to conflict events of tension, frustration, and aggression. This is an assumption based on the report of the Committee on Adolescence of the Group for the Advancement of Psychiatry (ages 10–20), included in *Normal Adolescence* (New York: Scribners, 1968). Youth are particularly involved in the intrapersonal conflict between their aggressive impulses and socially sanctioned norms of moral behavior. This internal condition usually leads to a projection of aggression externally. A sensitive planning for the constructive, effective use of this conflict could result in some considerable growth and development of the adolescent. Both verbal experiences and non-verbal exercises provide opportunities for the structuring of conflict, and for the working through of the affective dimensions of their inner conflict. Youth weekends, particularly, provide a natural laboratory for experiences of this nature. Most youth groups already have built-in conflicts which could be surfaced as the structured way for this education to take place. Sensitive management of this conflict can help them get in touch with their inner conflicts and learn better ways to handle conflict and to discover the possibilities for healing. This conflict may be staged as well using adults on such a weekend to utilize youth's aggressive tendencies as they deal with power imbalances at this particular time of their lives. Some of the issues of the generation gap can provide the subject for this structured conflict. This form can pick up on the feelings of youth, such as their felt limitations and alienation and their feelings of adult domination. Adults can then express their feelings of hard-earned advantages taken too lightly by youth, and the concern that history not be repeated by the current youth. The use of the generation gap for conflict and the utilization of that conflict for growth is a positive educational strategy in working with this age group.

Conflict can also be structured on such youth weekends by bringing together combinations of youth groups such as white suburban with inner city minority young people. Careful management and development of community is necessary for effective learning through this structuring of conflict. Specific planning for such youth weekends will also be considered in Part III of this book as we deal with specific procedures.

Another model describing the use of instructional conflict as the purposive, goal-directed structuring for learning can be found in this author's course on Conflict Management and Utilization taught in the seminary at The Iliff School of Theology in Denver, Colorado. The concern in such a course is preparation of pastors and other church leaders for the understanding and effective utilization of conflict in their profession. The design of this course begins with the student attempting to bring to consciousness or awareness the present state of intrapsychic conflict. Both theoretical material and exercises for action help begin this process of self-awareness of conflict within. The theoretical design reflects the conviction noted earlier that the intrapersonal conflict is the beginning and locus for the resultant interpersonal and intergroup conflict.

The course design moves out of the individual focus into the interpersonal and intergroup focus by further theoretical presentation along with the experience of exercises deliberately establishing conflict amongst the group members. Integrating experience and reflection with theoretical materials helps the individual see how his or her own intrapersonal conflict has become involved with the interpersonal, intergroup experience. Reflection and feedback time allows for the increased awareness of the dynamics of both individual and group experiences and the integration into self-understanding. The conclusion of the learning design allows for the selection of a conflict experience that the person is presently going through, usually in the church, and utilizes triads as a means of presenting, listening, and helping to focus on what events are taking place and what intrapersonal conflicts are reflected in this chosen conflict example. This is a means of moving from the uniqueness of the classroom community to the community in which individuals work in society. Structured conflict plays a role in each of the phases of this conflict course.

Each of the models which have been cited in this chapter

provides ways of understanding and utilizing the planned, deliberative, goal-directed, instructional use of conflict. More specific procedures from these models will be presented in the latter part of the book.

Notes

1. James Michael Lee, *The Shape of Religious Instruction* (Mishawaka, Ind.: Religious Education Press, 1971), p. 58.

2. James Michael Lee, "The Teaching of Religion," in *Toward a Future for Religious Education,* ed. J. M. Lee and P. C. Rooney (Dayton, Ohio: Pflaum Press, 1970), pp. 59–61.

3. Robert L. Conrad, "Creative Learning in Christian Education: A Model of Creative Conflict" (Paper given at the Association of Professors and Researchers in Religious Education meeting, St. Louis, Mo., Nov. 19, 1977).

4. Ibid., p. 2.

5. Ibid., pp. 4–7.

6. Ibid., p. 12.

7. B. Aubrey Fisher, *Small Group Decision-Making: Communication and the Group Process* (New York: McGraw-Hill, 1974), pp. 140–145.

8. Thomas Scheidel and Laura Crowell, *Discussing and Deciding: A Desk Book for Group Leaders and Members* (New York: Macmillan Publishing Co., 1979), pp. 160–189.

9. H. Edward Everding, Jr., Clarence H. Snelling, and Mary M. Wilcox, "Toward a Theory of Instruction for Religious Education" (Paper given at the meeting of the Association of Professors and Researchers in Religious Education, Washington, D.C., November 1976).

9 Structuring Conflict for Positive Human Functioning

The church has the potential for being an open and free organization based on individual self-worth and responsibility. With the allowance for individual uniqueness, we must expect people to differ in their ways of thinking and acting. That is both inevitable and desirable. Differences can be valuable and creative. If our differences are seen as God-given and unique, we need to provide opportunities to find the best from all. That puts heightened emphasis on making decisions from amongst a variety of solutions without infringing on others' freedom and individual autonomy. This may not always be possible to the satisfaction of all, and differences must find some reconciliation. I believe our goal is to have a creative, committed, problem-solving community.

If this community is to become a reality, the individuals in this community need to have an understanding of the roots of conflict and some skills in gaining resolution of differences. Problem-solving processes need to be creative and informed, with an individual sensitivity to our own behavior and the reactions of others to it. In order to acquire such understanding, both conceptual and personal, a considerable responsibility is lodged in the community for informative feedback. The need for self-understanding and skills for conflict resolution places a heavy responsibility on the Christian community. All persons involved in leadership in the church need the training and feedback on ways that will enable them to strengthen their own capacities and skills for coping with conflict. All leadership in the church have educational roles as our educational concept is pervasive throughout the church organization. Therefore, this chapter will give some modes of conflict resolution and structures for positive human functioning throughout the church organization.

The regulation of conflict becomes an important institutional concern if we are to deal constructively in our modes of resolution. If conflict is not regulated, it tends to bring ill-defined tensions and hostilities with the possibilities of violence and accidental solutions, if any at all. Avenues other than regulation may be such as suppression out of fear of control or redirecting to substitute areas and objects.

Regulation does have the possibility of facilitating some creative accords that could provide growth for individuals and the organization as a whole through the organizational structure. Institutionalized structures are most helpful in creating the conditions for constructive conflict utilization.

H. Wilson Yates gives us some guidelines as he reviews four conditions for an institution to structure, or regulate, conflict:

1. The organization must recognize the diversity of interests and goals within itself, having their commonality as well as their diversity. This is a positive recognition.
2. Conflict, when it arises, must be organized or regulated.
3. Voluntary associations must express interests and allow the organization an out-in-the-open expression of the varieties of interests. Opportunity to hear and to criticize must be included.

4. There should always be a general distribution of authority and exercise of power. All interests need to be pro-
   tected from domination of any one interest.[1]

These four conditions will help an institution to structure in
accommodation to internal conflict.

Yates also gives us some procedural factors that could be
helpful in structuring conflict for positive human functioning.
These factors include the following:

1. The issues and points of agreement within the community must be clarified for positive functioning.
2. There needs to be recognition of other positions in a
   way which allows individuals to get inside the opposite
   stance. A third party sometimes helps here. One could
   even use intellectual and empathetic situational role
   playing.
3. Factors leading up to the conflict need to be investigated
   to see if there may indeed be deeper roots to the present
   conflict.
4. A range of solutions deemed feasible by all is desirable.
   This will help to keep the conflict from being a
   pathological satisfaction meeting an individual's needs.[2]

These procedural factors will help conflict be dealt with constructively and move toward the benefit of the collective
interests.

Essentially what we are doing is finding ways of setting the
general situation in the church in such a way that when conflict does appear, it has the likelihood of being utilized constructively. In general, this situation finds members not necessarily pitted against one another in factions but rather arrayed
in a high degree of cohesion. Common goals are vital in

establishing an effective use of energy and resources of the congregation. This regulation emphasizes a cooperative climate in which the collective task is more important than the individual. This is not a sacrifice of the individual because the person finds his or her own needs merged into the collective task. Common needs and satisfactions are emphasized in contrast to highly individual ones.

This does require certain characteristic individual behavior in the community. This climate needs to be such within the Christian community that will foster such positive individual behavior. The following is a helpful characterization:

1. A cooperative attitude toward the collective goal.
2. Participation by all in discussion.
3. A basic community support for the presentation of the opinions of others. This feeling of support is basic for the success of such operation.
4. Reflective consideration before the presentation and defense of viewpoints. This includes the acknowledgment of the legitimacy of other points of view, allowing for all ideas to be examined by a similar method.
5. Personalities are not a part of the debate of issues and ideas.
6. A basic attitude toward disagreement as positive and as a useful means for gaining perspective.
7. A collective orientation which works toward compromise and searches for ways to resolve differences creatively.
8. An open and non-threatening climate of communication.[3]

Work in education toward such characteristic individual behavior would be an important part of the educational program of the whole church. This type of individual behavior does not just happen. It needs educating. Important ingredients in achieving these positive characteristics are individual self-worth and recognition, a need which all have. The effect of such education is the experience of high trust and friendliness with a new sense of realistic unity and security, not one which leads to the earlier mentioned concept of group-think which becomes unrealistic in its cohesive unity.

Problem Solving

Morton Deutsch proposes a hypothesis. He says that productive conflict resolution is similar to the process involved in problem solving or creative thinking. The characteristics of this process are as follows:

1. There is an initial period leading to the experiencing and recognition of a problem which is sufficiently arousing to motivate efforts to solve it.
2. A period of concentrated effort follows to solve the problem through routine available, or habitual, actions.
3. When customary processes fail to solve the problem, there is the experience of frustration and tension which leads to temporary withdrawal from the problem.
4. There is an incubation period allowing for distancing from the problem which allows for a differing perspective and a reformulation in a way that permits a new orientation for a solution to emerge.
5. A tentative solution appears in a moment of insight which often is accompanied by a sense of exhilaration and release.
6. The new solution is elaborated upon, detailed, and tested against reality.

7. Finally, the solution is communicated to the relevant audience.[4]

In order for creative problem solving to take place, an open, non-threatening climate must be present to ensure the feeling of self-esteem and self-worth for those affected by the change. Motivation to creative problem solving is also affected by the readiness of persons involved to be dissatisfied with things the way they are and a feeling of freedom to confront that environment without excessive fear and with self-confidence. Again, a feeling of self-worth is critical. Unresolved problems create tensions that may surface elsewhere. Constructive use of those tensions would be nearly impossible.

The Likerts refer to a similar style of problem solving in their steps for intellectual problem solving. They lift up some learned skills that need to be applied simultaneously:

1. Locate the problem and state it clearly. Be sure it is the real problem.
2. Define the conditions or criteria which the solution must meet to be satisfactory. These are essential criteria. List other conditions desirable afterwards.
3. Search for all promising solutions. Try to use different frames of reference and ways of looking at the problem to develop new, better solutions (brainstorming).
4. Obtain all relevant facts for the extent to which each solution would meet the criteria and also the desirable effects.
5. Evaluate all suggested solutions in terms of the criteria and desirable effects.
6. Select the solution which best meets the criteria. Eliminate first the solutions that don't meet the criteria of

essential conditions, then eliminate progressively those which meet desirable conditions least satisfactorily.

7. Check the solution finally selected over against the problem as stated to be sure it really solves the problem. Also check for bad side effects.[5]

Notice that an important term has been advanced here—intellectual problem solving. The emotional dimension cannot be ignored, however. If there is basic distrust, for example, intellectual activity will go poorly. There is the danger of a hidden agenda, and the real goals and objectives may never be truly faced.

An important shift to constructive problem solving can be seen when sincere, supportive behavior is exhibited by leadership and followed by the group membership. Supportive relations shown by group leadership can make for more effective procedures in the intellectual problem-solving experience. When something is being said in the group, it must be felt to be important even if it is not agreed with. The leader can show this type of supportive listening and lift it up for the group to follow. We are again emphasizing the point of self-esteem and self-worth to be a critical factor if creative problem solving is to take place. Supportive listening can be imposed upon the group by a leader. It is the exercise of requiring the re-stating of another's position and reasons for it before speaking to the point.

Another emphasis critical to creative problem solving is work toward integrative goals which express the deep-seated needs and desires of the conflicting parties and which bring them together toward mutually acceptable solutions. Without commitment to common objectives or integrative goals, there will be very little sacrificing of personal well-being for the organization. The task of leadership is to make integrative goals operationally effective in helping to resolve conflict. The task will vary according to whether goals are clearly present and accepted or are present but not yet explicitly recognized. Leadership has responsibility for seeing that the integrative goals that are potentially or implicitly present become explicit and fully recognized, accepted, and worked toward.[6]

One of the mistakes that we often run into in the church and other organizations is falling back on Robert's Rules of Order to solve differences. The result often takes the form of a technical solution and not one that resolves the issues in the group. A win/lose process results. We affirmed earlier that a win/win lifestyle is most effective and desired and particularly consistent with the values of the Christian community. Work toward consensus seems much more valuable, although frequently more difficult. We must aim toward a sense of the gathering in which free and open exchange takes place until consensus. Each viewpoint must be heard and considered. The conclusion may not be the exact wishes of each participant but rather an incorporation of the common objectives of all in a way that does not violate anyone. Achieving consensus in problem solving stresses a cooperative effort to find a sound solution acceptable to everyone, rather than a competitive struggle in which an unacceptable solution is forced on the losers.[7]

Certain conditions must be worked for if one truly expects consensus making to work. The following outline lists conditions associated with high consensus in groups of either substantive or affective conflict:

1. There is little inclination to express personal, self-oriented needs.

2. When self-needs are expressed, these needs are satisfied during the course of the meeting.
3. There is a general pleasant atmosphere in which participants recognize the need for unified action.
4. The problem-solving activity needs to be understandable, orderly, and focused on one issue at a time.[8]

These conditions can be met with leadership who know how to structure conflict positively, utilizing the forces of the conflict so that persons are challenged to grow by their differences rather than pressed to take defense of their being and worth. Problem solving by consensus will not allow organizational leadership to rely on the easy win/lose, majority rule conclusion, but rather makes us work with our theological conviction of individual worth as a gift of God.

Notes

1. H. W. Yates, "A Strategy for Responding to Social Conflict," *Pastoral Psychology* 22, no. 216 (1971): 38–40.

2. Ibid., p. 40.

3. Gerald M. Phillips, Douglas J. Pedersen, and Julian T. Wood, *Group Discussion: A Practical Guide to Participation and Leadership* (Boston: Houghton-Mifflin Co., 1979), p. 67.

4. Morton Deutsch, "Conflicts: Productive and Destructive," in *Conflict Resolution through Communication,* ed. Fred E. Jandt (New York: Harper and Row, 1973), pp. 171–172.

5. Rensis and Jane Likert, *New Ways of Managing Conflict* (New York: McGraw-Hill, 1976), p. 126.

6. Ibid., pp. 141–142.

7. Ibid., p. 146.

8. Ibid., p. 148.

10 Structuring Conflict
for Enhancing Self-Acceptance
and Reconciliation

The concept and dynamics of both self-acceptance and reconciliation were cited earlier in the theoretical portion of this book as being crucial for the climate necessary for the best utilization of conflict for the individual. Both self-acceptance and reconciliation are a difficult dynamic to bring about and require the assistance of a supportive community such as we have in the context of the Christian community. For oftentimes we only partially have the desire to know who we are in order to accept who we are and find reconciliation that is possible in such a context. Self-understanding ties closely together with the intention to know ourselves and the motivation to find self-acceptance and reconciliation. Our reluctance to face ourselves is sometimes reflected in the flight each of us has taken from our awareness of guilt—guilt from which we try to flee, rather than come to know. There must be some framework which will allow us to embrace our guilt or acceptance of ourselves as we are, and then to be liberated to embrace our possibilities. This is a tension which has been researched by John Haught in his book *Religion and Self-Acceptance*.

Theologically, this self-acceptance and reconciliation are described as gifts from God which we refer to as the "experience of grace." After the experience of grace, one begins to sense the depths of personal freedom. Freedom from a judgmental "other" which watches, approves, and condemns, is necessary in order to restore the sense of self, self-desire, self-freedom. With the sense of a hovering "other," we feel the need to develop self-deception in order to overcome our shortcomings, our guilt, and our rebellion. We deceive ourselves into a psychic immobility and blame it upon this God. There develops a most deep sense of distance between our desires and spontaneity and the corresponding will of God. We constantly need to sacrifice our wants to what He wants. When we develop a spontaneity, we immediately are covered by feelings of guilt analogous to those Freud illustrates in the superego/id battle.[1] John Haught contends that the reason we have difficulty with our self-acceptance and reconciliation is that we are afraid to associate ourselves with our desire to know. He affirms this basic desire to know as good and leading to the possibility of self-acceptance and reconciliation. This inner conflict is a basic problem for each of us. We must solve the ambiguity within ourselves in order to avoid the projection of this inner ambiguity onto others in interpersonal conflict.

It is Haught's contention that the coercive deity of Theism must be transcended in one's religious development so that there is no longer any trouble from the fear of deep desires coming into conflict with an external source of norms for thought and action. If this threat can be overcome without guilt or repression, our strivings can make their way to the surface. A new source of freedom and autonomy develops with the feeling of a new self-acceptance and reconciliation.[2] There is a need to feel that one's redemption is no longer a magical action from without, but rather an experience of what is called autonomy.

One's acceptance and reconciliation are bound together in a religious story for the Christian, the story of God's Son's experience with mankind expressed in the New Testament. An example of this freeing action through the story of Jesus is seen in the conversion of Paul. Paul experienced unconditional acceptance from a God who once had held him captive in the law. God accepted him in spite of the evil and inadequacy which Paul was never able to shake under the law. The law and his lack of freedom created Paul's need for self-deception. The law was necessary because of our domination by desires, other than the pure desire to know. In Paul's experience, it was coming to know the story of the God of unconditional, accepting love that enabled him to look more deeply into himself than ever before, allowing for the experience of self-acceptance and reconciliation. His prior efforts had been toward self-justification. He, like others after him, was caught in his inability to live up to the ideals projected by the law. In Christianity, Paul found the story that best expressed his own innermost feelings. This gave Paul a new freedom from the "cover story" that his fanatical Pharisaism had made for him. This self-deception prohibited him from using his energies in free expression, needing them to fuel his combat within. This new freedom released Paul from his intrapsychic conflict and allowed for a new spontaneity of life reflected in his self-acceptance and inner reconciliation. It is Haught's conviction that the acceptance of the self requires some story which can reshape the person. That religious story was the story of Christ for Paul. Prior to the acceptance possible through the religious story, it is most difficult for anyone to look deeply within the self openly and with the possibilities of no self-deception. The need is for the self-acceptance which can release the feelings and desires previously felt unacceptable, yet truly you. In Christianity, it is the story of God's unconditional love which promotes or allows the quest for truthfulness toward one's self, or self-acceptance. It eliminates the fear of our darker side. We can finally imagine being accepted whatever our case. Nothing that we do or do not do can change this basic conviction. There is no longer any need to hide. The past is accepted along with the present. The only barrier, then, is our refusal to accept this possibility as ours. This refusal, when taken, is rooted in our ultimate will to power and desire for mastery.[3]

It is making that circle which leads us back to Tillich's concept of anxiety and our basic need for reconciliation with self, each other, and with our God. It is our gratitude to our God who has created us which can save us from our restlessness and non-acceptance of ourselves. Participation, then, in the religious story which is Christianity, in the Yes by God to persons on the basis of friendship rather than coercion, provides for us the symbolic basis for the sincere Yes to ourselves.

Structuring for Enhancement

Change is a constant, it has been said. In our modern day, change is occurring at a rate faster than we have ever experienced in our society. Change produces conflict, particularly when it is handled in a win/lose way of problem solving. There has been considerable research on change in organizations, and much has been developed which shows the potential of the win/win methodology in meeting problem-solving needs in organizations. We have the usual causes of conflict with struggles for power, desire for economic gain, need for status, and exploitation of others. These have been with us in the secular organization, and they have also been with us in the church organization. When there is such change, human needs increase in the area of security needs. Tensions increase and so does the defensive reaction. Our need is for the discovery of methods of resolving problems constructively without eliminating the creative differences which exist amongst us as we go through change.

It has been discovered that higher levels of creativity are found in organizations which deliberately stimulate innovative-mindedness by encouraging diversity and differences amongst their people. This approach shakes people out of comfortable ruts and makes possible new thinking. This experience can be negative unless it is well managed.

Social science research has discovered factors in conflict management which produce an effective system. This research has been mostly on the productivity of business as a system. It has been discovered, however, that such a system works better under volunteerism than under the profit motive. The Likerts have brought this research together and have described the system as System 4. This highly effective system takes the important question of self-acceptance and self-worth as the basis for its operation. In this sense, System 4 has been tested as one of the most highly effective structures for organizations interested in the utilization of conflict based on the central part of this book—self-worth.

The main ingredients of this system are:

1. The nature of supportive leadership.
2. Integrative goals and supportive behavior.
3. De-emphasis on status and depersonalization of problem solving.
4. An interacting network of linked pins.
5. Consensus making and win/win problem solving.[4]

Yes, this does relate to our subject of structuring conflict to enhance self-acceptance and reconciliation. This system is based on the human need for satisfactory control over one's life and destiny. People need to be able to feel they can influence decisions which affect them. Each of us needs to feel we have worth and importance. The degree to which these basic needs are met relates to the degree of effectiveness of the social system used for enhancing self-acceptance and self-worth, particularly during conflict. We must allow time for the building of an effective system in order for it to be ready to use when conflicts do appear. Let us look at the variables for constructing a system that will utilize conflict for the enhancing of self-acceptance and reconciliation.

SUPPORTIVE LEADERSHIP

Research indicates that the greater amount of supportive behavior contributes to greater success in resolving cross functional conflicts constructively and in achieving effective integration in an organization. Also, confrontation in dealing with conflict helped higher performing organizations. It was the supportive relationships which were critical, however. The leader must behave so that each member feels that his/her experience is a supportive one and one which builds and maintains a sense of personal worth and importance.[5]

This description is directly contrary to the pattern we are most familiar with called win/lose. This win/lose pattern of organizational interaction is characterized by factions which are immediately set off against each other to win for one and lose for the other. Close group cohesion develops in each as they close ranks against the other. Leadership concentrates and power structure establishes itself quickly within each group. As conflict grows, there is less time for participation and deliberation amongst members, and diversity must be sacrificed for unity. This creates future intragroup conflict as well as intergroup conflict. Judgmental and perceptual distortions occur as to the qualities of each group. Everything is ranked as superior versus inferior and objectivity declines. Information is distorted in the exchange in both intellect and memory. Similarities and commonalities are overlooked, and minute differences take on great importance. The pressure in such a system is not to be objective or innovative or seek the best solution. It is to win at any cost.[6]

The win/lose structuring of conflict contains two powerful motivating forces. The first is a desire for physical security, and the second is the desire to achieve and maintain a sense of personal worth and importance. When these two desires are threatened, an intense emotional reaction is bound to follow. The problem results from the fact that all parties, or at least the two parties providing the conflict, take a very clear solution from the start and try to impose it upon the other. They fail to create a problem-solving orientation which reaches for a best possible solution for both parties. A bargaining, negotiating, compromising attitude prevails. Such structuring does not provide for the enhancement of self-acceptance or reconciliation.[7]

The need for conflict utilization in the church and elsewhere is for a system which is both growth oriented and effective, effective both in task performance as well as group maintenance. The leadership and organizational climate are important variables in providing such effective group experience. Other variables which are important to conflict management need to be included as well. Such variables as capacity to communicate, to motivate, to coordinate, and to influence will be necessary for good conflict management. If such variables are working well, decision making will be a positive experience. Problems should be detected early because of the communication and solved promptly. There will be an overlapping in the group structure which provides for the communication necessary in problem solving and assures involvement of those affected. Decisions are made by the group utilizing integrative goals rather than by hierarchical individuals with personal needs and goals. Decisions that are reached will be well carried out because of the involvement of all.

Leadership of a group that utilizes conflict will necessarily be very supportive and friendly, listening to what others are saying with obvious attention. Leadership will be team building, encouraging all to work together in exchange of ideas and support of one another's attempts throughout the group structure. The leader will encourage all to work on goals and to maintain high standards in the achievement of goals. The basic role for such leadership is showing a concern for persons, their self-worth and their importance in the organization. The ideas of all are respected, even though they differ and may be disagreed with, but they are deemed important and worked through.

As in any good group, the members engage in leadership behavior, and if the group leader has exhibited the values and style previously described, the group members will be able to follow such leadership example. They, too, will provide support for other members in their sense of worth and importance in the group. They will be able to provide for facilitation of interaction which affects both group maintenance and the group task. Goal emphases will be kept in the fore, such that members find the group goals in close proximity to their individual goals. The concern for the church is for good lay leadership, and if pastoral leadership is able to provide the style and the values for the lay leadership, these should be pervasive throughout the church organization.

There is a basic need for understanding small group behavior and leadership if pastors are to provide this kind of group experience and example for lay leadership. All too often the church experiences the pastoral leadership as individual and lacks any serious involvement or organizational climate that has been described here.

I wish to underscore the need for supportive leadership in the church. Each member must be able to view his/her experience in the group or the church as a supportive one and one which builds and maintains a sense of personal worth and value. Members find self-acceptance and reconciliation exemplified in the pastoral leadership as well as amongst their peers in the church organization. If this is their experience, it will lead to motivation, cooperation, and effective behavior throughout the organization. It is important to be reminded again that we are not talking about a way of lessening conflict in the church. The concern here is that differences be valued, and that those differences find an effective way of enhancing the organization and the individuals within it. We are not trying to block conflict from the church, but to find ways of valuing our God-given uniqueness and difference and to find effective ways of utilizing those differences into creative problem solving and innovative behavior throughout the church organization and its mission. We are attempting to structure conflict into effective, facilitating organizational behavior, both within and without. This attempt is based upon the premise that all persons have a strong, inherited desire to achieve and to maintain a sense of personal worth and acceptance. They must be helped to the point of self-acceptance. Leadership must be able to be aware of how others perceive themselves and are perceived, and must know how to help people change behavior according to their desire and their needs. Feedback becomes very important for the leader, as well as for the members within the group, for our perception of what is going on is not necessarily the fact of the experience of each person. The aim for good leadership here is to help persons to interact and to achieve and maintain a sense of personal worth that leads to self-acceptance and reconciliation. To behave in such a way requires both leadership and membership to have a basic faith in persons and a generous attitude toward others. They must have confidence in their abilities, judgment, and integrity, and have trust for them and for one another. This finds theological base in the presence of the Spirit in every one of us in our uniqueness and in our need to make contribution for the good of the whole. Faith in the presence of the Spirit in each one and in his/her unique contribution is an important assumption for leadership in the church. That assumption must be spread throughout the membership for effective utilization of each's gift to the whole.[8] A critical dimension of the Christian community is the understanding of all involved that the relationships which they provide are the medium through which persons find their self-worth and self-acceptance, receive the feedback necessary for growth, experience the trust to take risks, and find that through their relationships they are able to experience the working of the Holy Spirit through themselves and others.

It is important to understand that this concept of leadership and peer facilitation is not to create the image of the leader as a nice guy who merely keeps people happy. It is rather the image of the leader providing a high standard of expectation for their participation and involvement, for their creativity and leadership. All too often, pastors do a good job of facilitating their own leadership and only pacifying people in the process. This makes the membership feel weak, incompetent, and inferior. They do not feel significant nor valued except as they back the pastoral leadership. This begins a process of creating conflict which is kept beneath the surface and is liable to explode at any time. Members need to feel significant and accepted. They also need to feel that their mission is important and that they can make valuable contributions to it. The role of the leader becomes important in bringing this about. The leadership must foster creativity and innovation, participation in planning, and ownership in the direction, the working, and the future of the organization. Conflict is inevitable when persons feel significant and free. The structuring of the organizational climate, the supportive role of leadership will help to take that conflict and to turn its energy and creative force back into the organization for its growth as well as for the growth of the individuals who are a part of it.

When this leadership and organizational climate are not present, when the structure does not enhance self-acceptance and reconciliation, a defensive atmosphere can be expected and the sense of progress forward in growth will be inhibited. Threat and risk pervade the atmosphere, support is felt lacking, and the energy of persons within finds diversion to behavior which is defensive, sapping the problem-solving task. Thus begins the destructive climate which many experience in their organizations. If trust is lacking, information will be more controlled, and possibilities of deliberate miscommunication grow. Distortion and miscommunication foster conflict, and in such an atmosphere it is sure to develop destructively. Support allows for more freedom and experimentation with creative attitudes and ideas. It allows more testing and retesting of perceptions and opinions and support for each who gives them. A lack of support creates a sense of threat and anxiety and a loss of efficiency in processing the information that is there.[9]

The emphasis so far in structuring enhancement of self-acceptance and reconciliation has been on supportive relationships as the end and aim for leadership and on the effective procedure for problem solving throughout the organization. Problem solving as a process was outlined and emphasized in the previous chapter, as that process was used for enhancement of positive human functioning. In all, there has been a high degree of focus on the leadership as both the control factor and an example for group members in their leadership. It must be constantly emphasized that all conflict is not good. Leadership has the possibility of controlling whether the group can stand the level of conflict that is arising and where it needs to be controlled. It is also important that the leader be able to see the difference between conflict as mere trouble making and disagreement or as idea producing and potentially constructive.

INTEGRATIVE GOALS

A very important variable in constructive conflict utilization procedures that the Likerts' research indicates is that integrative goals, common values, and mutual interests are vital in the facilitating of constructive resolution of conflict.[10] Integrative goals are those which express the deep-seated needs and desires of the conflicting parties, and will bring them together to work on mutually acceptable solutions. With integrative goals, the best interests of all can be sought. It is not likely that individuals will sacrifice personal well-being without the feeling that the objectives that the group is after are self-enhancing and that they can find deep commitment to them as well. It is the task of group leadership to make the integrative goals operationally effective in helping to resolve conflict. The goals may not be clear at all and may need the help of leadership to bring this clarification and to become explicitly recognized and accepted. Without the ability to come to such integrative goals, serious problems will be faced in bringing conflict to creative use.

Basic human needs often become the basis for integrative goals. The sense of personal worth and significance ties in with the need of all for achievement, growth, recognition, fulfillment, self-actualization. With integrative goals, one can mitigate the effects of hostile attitudes that may arise in the process of problem solving. Supportive behavior and hostile behavior are at either end of an extreme. The leadership may have to show the individual members this incongruity if it is experienced within the group. Sometimes it can be valuable to tape record the process and to allow time for playback in order for members to become aware of the attitudes that they are advancing and experiencing.

With integrative goals, the group dynamic then is to move toward a consensus. This does not mean towards a vote using Robert's Rules of Order, which is a win/lose process, but rather a win/win style of group dynamic which allows each to feel that he/she is essential for the satisfactions of the group to be met and that the group's process is toward the satisfaction of all, not a few. Consensus becomes important at each step of the decision-making process, especially at the final solution. It involves a sense of all who are there, that the way they are moving is acceptable and leading toward fulfillment that they each require. The process involves a free and open exchange of ideas which continues until agreement can be reached. Each is heard and each is considered significant. The conclusion will not exactly satisfy all but it will not violate any, and all can find some parts of it which do satisfy them. This describes a cooperative effort to find a solution which will help all, rather than a competitive struggle to find a solution which will be the answer for some and create losers for others. Again, it will be the group leadership and the organizational climate which will make the difference. The structuring must be done and experienced before the conflict arises, such that it is there to work in the midst of conflict.[11]

Not all consensus will be complete. It may be necessary for there to be only partial consensus which would then allow for a place for some success to be experienced by the group. It can be a tentativeness toward a particular part of the concern of all which does have some agreement. There can be a time allowed for a trial run and for evaluation in order to make a start. Such partial consensus can build the trust and confidence necessary for the larger interaction toward solving the problem as a whole. If pragmatic consensus is not possible, then there needs to be a turning back to the basic search for stronger or additional integrative goals on behalf of the group. With stronger or more complete goals there may be the possibility of rediscovering an innovative solution which will meet the conditions needed by all. This process may be required more than just once. Importance is given to the leader who is working on consensus and his or her ability to provide for orderly group problem solving undertaken in a supportive atmosphere.

DE-EMPHASIS ON STATUS AND PERSONALITY

Another critical factor which the Likerts emphasize in such structuring for conflict utilization is that of de-emphasizing status and depersonalizing the problem-solving process.[12] The research points to the fact that hierarchical status can act as a strong deterrent on the membership of an organization in their feeling important enough to speak up with their ideas. This is a basic problem for pastors in their leadership of churches. It holds true for any designated leadership. It is unfortunate that many act unaware of the impact of this status. We often encounter leadership which actually strives for status, and in turn the leaders find they are in competition with group membership and hostile attitudes are created. A virtue such as humility belongs in a Christian community, but it has become one with which leadership has trouble when we take into account the basic need of persons to feel important and to have status. The degree to which leadership within the church strives for status is the degree to which that organization will find conflict created that will be destructive and not constructive. Reconciliation and self-worth will be a goal most difficult to attain.

Supportive leadership concerned about membership experience of self-acceptance and worth as well as reconciliation will find it important to depersonalize differences that are experienced within the group and to remove the identification of ego from contributions of members. Proposals or contributions can be referred to in terms other than the name of the person who has given the proposal and allow, rather, for the group to take ownership of ideas. Individuals must be recognized for their contribution originally, but then it becomes the possession of the group as a whole. Data need to become depersonalized and objective. It can also be valuable to depersonalize the gathering of facts that become necessary for problem solving. Coordination of data gathering will be helpful to keep from the problem of building factional orientation in the problem-solving process. Each step needs to have participation by all in order that there is not single party ownership and direction to any part of the process.

We have not talked much about third party or referee style leadership. It can be utilized very effectively when needed. If pastoral or other organizational leadership is not available because of deep commitment to a single part or party in the process, then a third party does become important. This can be necessary in highly emotional situations. Use of a third party can allow for more acceptance of differences, better listening with understanding, and evaluation freed of bias. A third party can help clarify perceptions and the nature of the issue in ways that those who are deeply involved cannot. A third party can recognize and accept feelings such as fear, jealousy, and anger, and help the group deal with them, therefore maintaining the important relationships necessary to make progress and growth.

We can often find ourselves very task oriented in such organizations as the church. We may tend, then, to push things faster than individuals or the group may be ready to do, and run the danger of the resentment for "railroading." We need to remember group maintenance as well as the group task, and remember also that there is danger in getting to solutions before the problem has had sufficient time to be defined or fully exposed. Leadership continually needs to be concerned about structuring feedback into the process at all points.

Linkages

A key factor for the Likerts in facilitating an interaction influence network is a concept called linked multiple overlapping groups. This provides for individuals to be in linked relationship in subgroups within the larger organization. These linked pins provide a communication flow and influence throughout the whole which makes for reciprocal influence between groups in the larger organization. These link pins are not representatives, and as such do not have to represent the opinions, work, and attitude of groups that they are in, but rather provide for an important flow of information and ownership in the sense of the whole. This process helps keep tabs on the statement of the problem, the facts that go along in the development of the solution, knowledge of situational requirements, and awareness of the differences in conflicts that are encountered. The link pins have the role of mobilizing the motivational forces and focusing them on the constructive, cooperative problem solving. The focus or advantage of the link pins is their ability to exert influence in two or more directions, finding acceptance in various groups in the organization, and feeling psychologically closer to each group. They have the ability to communicate effectively with more than one group, knowing the vocabulary, values, and goals of each. They are therefore able to coordinate and enable differing groups to reach compatible solutions. What is even more important, they tend to create reciprocal responsibility for the implementations of decisions which are reached jointly. The overall effect of link pins is their ability to lead to the coordination of the total organization. This will lead to a more effective interaction influence network and to the capacity to resolve conflicts constructively.[13]

Win/Win Problem Solving

Power was treated as an important part of the theory portion of this book. It also becomes an important ingredient for understanding how to structure the organization for enhancing self-acceptance and reconciliation. It has already been established that power is the capacity to influence behavior. In a win/lose situation, that means that someone will exert power and influence toward their own personal ends. There will be those, then, who have power and those who are without it. In a win/win situation, which is a climate we have been referring to in this chapter, power stays in a fair state of equilibrium that will allow for a beneficial experience for all. This is not especially an individual sense of power but a sense of group power instead.

The power of the group is derived from individuals affirming the goals of the group and giving strength through their desire to achieve and maintain their sense of personal worth and importance. If individuals feel that their values are consistent with the group, that they are valued by that group, then the group takes on a new sense of power from all involved. The capacity of individuals within the group is to influence others and they feel that power of influence because they feel valued by the others of the group. Their self-worth, which is extended by the group, allows for their own sense of self-acceptance and reconciliation, freeing them to participate fully and openly and with the sense of satisfaction that is necessary for each. There is a variance of capacity within individuals within the group, but the group feeling tone is reciprocal or mutual. As the group power grows, it does not benefit one party at the expense of another. This is contrary to the variance of individual power in a win/lose situation. When the group experiences increasing power in the win/win situation, all parties within feel that increase and it becomes a part of their individual fulfillment. This increases the problem-solving potential of the group and both task and maintenance factors are strengthened. The basic difference exhibited shows a shift from using power over others to using joint power with others. This power then helps resolve conflicts with creative possibilities rather than destructive ones.[14]

It has been established that self-acceptance is a basic

psychological need and that reconciliation is a basic theological need. The dynamics and the process of achieving each have been referred to and developed in relation to the utilization of conflict. The structuring of an organization for effective use of conflict has come from much research, and in particular, from the writing of the Likerts. This structuring, if taken seriously by church leadership, can prove most effective in both task and group maintenance and facilitate the whole mission of the church by effectively utilizing the God-given differences which are a part of each of us as individuals. Such differences can provide for creative problem solving when utilized effectively and further the mission of the church in the community. When these differences are not effectively utilized, they create a breakdown in the mission, both within and without the church organization. Where there is such potential for positive use, we cannot afford to overlook concern for such structuring within the church as an organization.

Notes

1. John F. Haught, *Religion and Self-Acceptance* (New York: Paulist Press, 1976), pp. 158–159.

2. Ibid., pp. 163–164.

3. Ibid., pp. 171–173.

4. Rensis and Jane Likert, *New Ways of Managing Conflict* (New York: McGraw-Hill, 1976), p. 7.

5. Ibid., pp. 54–55.

6. Ibid., pp. 65–66.

7. Ibid., pp. 67–68.

8. Ibid., pp. 107–117.

9. Ibid., pp. 123–124.

10. Ibid., p. 141.

11. Ibid., pp. 142–147.

12. Ibid., pp. 157–177.

13. Ibid., pp. 183–200.

14. Ibid., pp. 269–282.

11 Structuring Conflict for Enhancing Affective Instruction

Two Functions of the Mind

Education for most of its history has focused upon the cognitive dimension or product orientation in its work. Focus has been on the imparting of knowledge, particularly that knowledge that we wish to selectively maintain from history as well as in the recent discovery of new knowledge. A part of the new knowledge that has come from educational research has been that the brain has two hemispheres, with each hemisphere having a differing function. That hemisphere on which we have been most dependent in our education is the left side of the brain, which processes the cognitive dimension, or the more intellectual domain. This would include the logical, analytical, more knowledge-comprehension activities including synthesis and evaluation. The right side of the brain processes the more affective dimension which would include such things as the intuitive, imaginal, metaphorical, creative, artistic, symbolic, emotional elements. Our attitudes, values, and beliefs in religion are vitally affected by this dimension of our brain's activity, even though they may be instructed by the left side of our brain.

It should be quite apparent that religious education has

great interest in the affective domain in education. However, our history proves that we, like other educational concerns, have focused on the cognitive dimension. We have been concerned that persons learn the content of the faith—its history, its traditions, the scriptural passages, and the moral evaluations which set the standard for the Christian lifestyle. We have been heavily verbally oriented until some of the influence from such sources as Marshall McLuhan's work found relationship to education as a whole. The recent attraction of Eastern forms of religious experience have made it all too clear that our cognitive focus has lost a very important dimension of the person's religious experience. The new interest in meditation, in Zen Yoga and transcendental meditation, coupled with new occultism and consciousness expansion, reflects an anti-cognitive movement in our Western culture. For many, it is a new discovery to learn that many of these affective dimensions to religion had been a very important part of the practice of the Christian faith. Our recent Western history has subtly left them out in the transmission and practice over the centuries. Our omission is now showing up in the interest in Eastern forms of religion.

A NEW BALANCE

The future looks like it might move toward a balance of the cognitive and affective dimensions for our culture and our educational developments. The possibility of creative achievements is enhanced by the combination of the two sides of the brain. There are attempts already for synthesizing these two modes of learning in our psychological research, in particular, the area of the science of human consciousness. Those in religious education are particularly interested in how this research develops, as they seek further to understand the process of religious development. A study of our Christian heritage would show a swing of the pendulum from the mystical, intuitive to the logical, rational emphasis for the church.

It is my concern here that we find a way of recognizing that education is both affective and cognitive, and that the experience of conflict is a dynamic that does integrate both hemispheres of the brain. It is when we try to deal with conflict with only one or the other side that we experience difficulties. The rational and the emotional dimensions must be included in our attempts at utilizing the experience of conflict.

CONFLUENCE

If in our education we are to move from our over-emphasis on logical, informational processing, we must become aware of the dynamic of confluence. If we expect internalization to be accomplished for learning, we need to include both sets of functions of the brain in relation to the content. This synthesizing function allows for integration of information and the formation of meaning together. Such a process, called confluence, brings together the rational, logical, informational data with metaphorical and imaginal processing. If we ignore the confluent process, we may get cognitive knowledge but find that the primal images relating to the concepts are not fashioned together, allowing conflict to develop within the learner.[1] In general, we are going to have to increase our planning and strategy for holistic education which allows for the complete person to be involved in the learning process. This is not to say that we go overboard on the affective side as we have on the cognitive. It is merely an attempt to achieve balance.

My concern here is to show how conflict can have advantage in the enhancement of the affective instruction, but it must be kept in mind that the cognitive dimension is to be in balance for the whole. Each has its place, both the presenting of the message as well as the experience of the effect and the affect, but it is the non-verbal area in our teaching/learning that needs to be brought up to balance with the verbal. There are teaching methodologies which can be developed which are primarily non-verbal and which can be used in conjunction with or in confluence with the cognitive dimensions of the same subject. I am particularly speaking of religious education as my concern in this chapter. This emphasis very obviously directs us to the student-centered instruction, rather than subject-centered instruction. The classroom has the possibility of becoming a learning community in which both teacher and learner become a vital part of the affective education experience in particular.

In furtherance of the confluent process, the research of the team of Everding, Snelling, and Wilcox, from The Iliff School of Theology, proposes a dialogical relationship between text, or subject if you will, and the interpreter (learner). This interpretive model is a confluent process. Everding, Snelling, and Wilcox make reference to Piaget's learning process involving the twin elements of assimilation and accommodation. Both must take place in order for the learning to be complete. New information must be accompanied by new understanding and internalization in order to avoid imbalance or distortion. This assimilation/accommodation relationship must move toward equilibration in order for optimal learning to be complete.[2]

Affective education is of particular concern for religious education as we look to the "subject" of attitude and values. It is very clear for everyone that the social climate set by teacher and student alike correlates significantly with attitude formation and value gain. The teacher's attitudes have considerable importance as to the learning of attitudes and values in the social climate of the classroom. Considerable attention needs to be paid to the interpersonal skills of a teacher in the setting of such a climate. Conflict is a vital part of the interpersonal dynamics of a classroom, and skills need to be learned to utilize this dynamic for positive gain.

AFFECTIVE EDUCATION FOR YOUTH

We learn as whole persons. This is a basic premise that has been established thus far. We need to be as interested in the feeling as we are in the doing and the rational dimension of the person. This holds true particularly in relation to the growth and development of adolescents. Their well-known personality conflicts of dependence-independence set them as prime targets for affective needs. Youth seem to respond more affectively to conflict events of tension, frustration, and aggression than adults. This is an assumption based on a report of the Committee on Adolescence of the Group for the Advancement of Psychiatry (ages 10–20).[3]

In our early section on theory, it was established that interpersonal conflict dynamics stem from intrapersonal conflict. This is an important understanding to be applied to the problem of youth and the education of youth. Internally, youth are plagued with the intrapersonal conflict between aggressive impulses and socially sanctioned norms of moral behavior. This intrapersonal dynamic is projected out onto those with whom they relate. This is particularly the case for the interrelationship between youth and parents and youth and their adult teachers. The normal climate for youth at home or in the classroom is to experience a discrepancy in power between themselves and the adults. Our religious education planning needs to take this into account and develop a cooperative rather than a competitive structure to be most helpful for the youth in dealing with this inner conflict. The training of teachers and leaders in the art of affective education and skills for non-verbal communication could be an important concern in furthering the educative use of this basic inner conflict in youth. After all, as William Glasser writes in his *Schools without Failure,* Reality Therapy says there are two basic human needs: 1) the need for love, 2) the need for self-worth.[4] This obviously calls for more concern directed to affective goals in our educational planning.

Structuring expresses a theory for instruction which was referred to earlier. It is common knowledge in teaching that you can either structure for uncooperative relationships or you can structure for cooperative social relationships in the classroom. Such dynamics relate vitally to the use of conflict in affective education. The advantage of structuring for uncooperative relations is that you can divide and rule. It is a major way of maintaining control in the classroom. This will foster conflict, distrust, and disorganization amongst the students. This produces more destructive conflict than constructive. It usually involves a multi-level status hierarchy for control of the classroom. Collaboration as a style is rarely achieved.

Structuring for cooperative social relationships works for a positive social climate and a social product. Control is still of concern, but it is channeled through areas of cooperation. Trust and loyalty are important dynamics to be established in such cooperative social relationships.

AN EXERCISE MODEL

Skills for using non-verbal communication are an important concern in the furthering of educative uses of conflict, particularly for affective educational concerns. For instance, it would be creative to utilize a non-verbal exercise for youth to experience the affective dimension of their inner conflicts. An example would be the use of what is called the Fingertip Exercise on Power. It is possible to experience kinetic energy, dominance/passivity, personal space, competition/cooperation, and control, and then discuss them in order to get to the tap root of this inner conflict of adolescence. It is the opportunity to experience both the negative and positive awareness of the use of their power. Psychological, social, and theological dimensions can be sorted out through this experience for perspective and individual growth. The actual inner conflict becomes the subject matter for learning and growth. For much too long, the church has been a part of the problem of this inner conflict for youth. As long as the church is a part of the problem, it need not expect youth to give loyalty, service, and devotion. The church does have the potential to be part of the solution, but first it must recognize the condition, accept it as valid, real, and important to deal with as a part of Christian growth.

The use of the Fingertip Exercise on Power can demonstrate a model for teaching learning that I think to be of great benefit in the church. It is an example of the rhythm of moving from theory to experience (exercise). Following the exercise, debriefing can take place with personal integration and acceptance of the new material in a supportive climate set by both teacher and fellow students. Basic problems of anxiety and hostility can be dealt with through such movement. Ontological needs can come forth and find support in the midst of a Christian community newly discovered through experiential exercises and debriefing. Two basic human needs can be rediscovered: love and self-worth, affirmed through the life of the classroom community as well as the larger organization of the church.

Actually, this model is applicable to the needs of adults as well. They need to be able to work out the dynamics of power that will be used in the Christian community at whatever level of organizational life. You can see the potential that such exercises have in growth groups in the church. A sense of personal space and worth, personal and ontological relations, authority and leadership and followership are all valid questions to be dealt with in such exercises. Learning how to utilize the conflict dimension in that experience for individual competitive ends or group cooperative ends is positive educative benefit. Task-oriented groups in the church structure also need help in order to do their job better. Structures, however, must be flexible enough to handle destructive conflict and change it over into constructive experience for growth and learning for all concerned.

With all the church's concern to learn the way of love and communication, it must not fail to recognize realistically the presence of hostility and learn to accept its presence. The liturgy is one point of the gathering of the community where hostility can be worked through, psychologically and theologically. The supremacy of God is recognized there, along with God's complete acceptance of each of us in grace over our imperfections of life. Our hostilities and anxieties can be experienced and conflict resolved through the faith process. Counseling in the church is another place to work through our basic, ambiguous hostilities, utilizing the transference process with a counselor in order to work through our ontological needs. I have already mentioned that children and youth need acceptance for this element of their growth, instead of learning how to repress hostility, becoming defensive with the church and the gospel as they grow. Married couples need help in dealing with their hostilities as well, rather than just feeling guilt when they fail at the model of the loving Christian.

Correct Answer Syndrome

Another dimension of this affective educational concern can be viewed under the title of the "correct answer syndrome."[5] This syndrome leads persons to a low tolerance of ambiguity. Such low tolerance leads to the experience of more conflict and a poorly developed interpersonal competence in relating to other human beings. We are especially in need of such interpersonal skills in order to discover the true potential of the Christian community. We need such competence in order to utilize conflict to achieve constructive results. If we are to be dependent on one another for help in discovering our God-given gifts and potential through the Christian community, and then develop them, we must have some laboratory for affective education and interpersonal skills.

In this time of great change, the tendency is to look for the correct answer. This is a time of increasing conservatism in our religious belief structures, showing a low tolerance for ambiguity. We are setting the stage for increasing destructive use of conflict in our churches with this climate. This very ambiguity and conflict which leads to a felt need for the "right answers" can become the very dynamics which, if creatively used, can lead to creative, affective education. The social climate for community experience can make the difference.

Simulation Games and Exercises

Reference was made to exercises as a base for getting at affective education. Most simulation games or exercises are based on issues coming from the allocation of limited resources or the intentional use of conflict as a way of gaining personal insight leading to personal growth. These exercises, or games, are a positive aid for affective learning in the church and outside it. Values education, in particular, has made great use of games and exercises to provide insights into the self and the social system. What is more, this process is fun. Of course, there is a deprecation of this use of verbal and non-verbal games and exercises because learning is supposed to be serious. Such work ethic values in relation to education can prohibit some of the most effective learning that is available. Such games and exercises can help people in the search for self-affirmation and self-worth. The basic struggle we have affirmed for humanity is the attempt at utilizing conflict as a positive force in life.

Simulations and exercises help structure conflict and have become a very important source for the integrative aspects of affective learning. Learners are provided with the opportunity to move from the cognitive theory to the safe practice of that cognitive learning in the midst of an accepting, loving community. Learners can actually try out the theory. Understandings can come about which are not available even with participatory discussion. There is the freedom to experiment with the new ideas, to try them on for size, and to learn how to evaluate them quickly for individual life and learning.

Such games and exercises provide a new educational technology. This includes the following:

1. All students have active and simultaneous participation in the learning experience.
2. The teacher is placed in the role of facilitator of the learning process, rather than the judge/controller.
3. Internal rather than external locus for rewards helps learner motivation by identifying and achieving personal goals rather than goals set by another.
4. The student is linked to the outside world through the simulation, reproducing in the setting of the classroom the conditions of regular life, allowing the practice of

various roles and decision making which the student will have to face in his or her lifestyle.[6]

This resource provides for a need that we will have in order to live in the future, that of learning how to grow, change, and integrate new experiences at increasing rates of speed. In the religious education process, a partnership can be created between teacher and student which will engage them in the process of problem solving and problem defining. Gaming can help diagnostic and analytic skills in relating to the world and to one another. It can help with coming to terms with power relationships which are a most critical dynamic in all conflicts. Simulations and exercises are basic conflict labs and can provide a means for teacher education as well as for student learning. The lab allows the person to have his or her perceptions checked by others and to be made aware of perceptions other than those he or she has experienced. This can be a very threatening experience unless there is that supportive feeling that his/her ideas and perceptions are accepted as they are. This is a true learning community. Theological reflection can follow such existential experience. It is a way of discovering that all experience has theological dimension and that all experience plays a part in faith development. Persons need to increase their experience in making theological meaning out of their daily experiences.

It should be understood that games and exercises are not necessarily complete in and of themselves. They are most often used in conjunction with other resources which may be religious education materials one would usually find. These would be readings, discussions, lectures, films, panels, and other content-producing instruments. This requires an important planning dimension of both cognitive and affective dimensions to the goals and objectives of lesson planning.

The use of games and exercises in affective religious education adds another dimension to the classroom which relates directly to affective learning. In the study of religious experience through psychology, Paul Pruyser has utilized the categories of psychological study to look at religious experience. They are the same categories as psychology applies to any experience. The categories of the perceptual, the linguistic, the emotional, the motor, are amongst those which Pruyser uses to analyze religious experience, or in fact, all experience.[7] These categories fit under the affective learning processes and are brought into the classroom through exercises and gaming. The psychology of religious experience is very much aware of how much religious experience depends upon the visual, the thought and language, the emotional and the motor, as well as the intellectual dimensions of human experience. If the classroom in religious education would take more seriously these affective means for teaching, the confluent educational concerns could be very adequately cared for.

Notes

1. H. Edward Everding, Jr., Clarence H. Snelling, and Mary M. Wilcox, "Toward a Theory of Instruction for Religious Education" (Paper given at the meeting of the Association of Professors and Researchers in Religious Education, Washington, D.C., November 1976), p. 14.

2. Ibid., p. 15.

3. Committee on Adolescence of the Group for the Advancement of Psychiatry, *Normal Adolescence* (New York: Scribner and Sons, 1968).

4. William Glasser, *Schools without Failure* (New York: Harper and Row, 1969), p. 12.

5. Allan D. Frank, "Conflict in the Classroom," in *Conflict Resolution through Communication,* ed. Fred E. Jandt (New York: Harper and Row, 1973), pp. 254–255.

6. Paul M. Dietterich, "Simulation-Games Theory and Practice in Religious Education," in *Foundations for Christian Education in an Era of Change,* ed. Marvin J. Taylor (Nashville: Abingdon Press, 1976), p. 157.

7. Paul Pruyser, *A Dynamic Psychology of Religion* (New York: Harper and Row, 1968).

PART III

CREATIVE CONFLICT AT THE POINT OF ACTION: SPECIFIC PROCEDURES

12 Specific Procedures for Using Creative Conflict in the Church

Conflict fulfills an inevitable component of our personal and organizational lives. Whenever you have persons and organizations with values, needs, wants, goals, and plans, there will be conflict. The issue is not, therefore, whether or not there will be differences leading to conflict, but rather how it will be utilized.

Conflict must be organized and regulated for constructive use. Its presence shows that change is going on or being resisted, and change could lead to growth. How? Conflict has destructive power to alienate persons and groups, stymie effective work in task groups, and temporarily frustrate the functioning of the supportive fellowship in the Christian community. It can also be of constructive assistance in dealing with critical issues and be a motivating source of energy for persons or groups.

What we most often miss in conflict situations is the understanding, the attitudes accompanying the skills that make it possible to utilize the dynamics creatively. Clergy and lay leadership need to develop appropriate skills to utilize conflict creatively in the church. Specific procedures could be shared to help in the midst of church life and work. I would like to use these last two chapters toward that end.

A crucial concern is to be able to identify conflict, deal with it openly and creatively, keeping it from being destructive of the ongoing Christian community. There are at least three elements present in nearly every church conflict: ineffective communication, threatened identity, and intransigence.[1] The key to making this conflict creative lies in successfully addressing each of these issues.

WARNING SIGNS AND CLARIFICATION

There are numerous procedures that have been outlined to help persons and groups deal creatively with the dynamics of conflict that would relate to the issues of communication, identity, and intransigence. Signs of emerging conflicts warn that unrest is present. Such "early warning" signs may be:

1. Sudden drop in attendance, with established members in particular
2. An increase in telephoning amongst the membership
3. Frequent resignations from positions of leadership
4. Polarization of opinions and the formation of factions[2]

Noting this development within a congregation directs this community to strategize or make some clarifying diagnoses. The following questions help the diagnosis:

1. Who are the people and factions involved?
2. What are the issues—those talked about as well as those felt?
3. What are the underlying causes?
4. What is the extent of the conflict? Are these wider issues and how "hard" are the positions already taken?

5. What are the priorities? How urgent is *this* conflict in comparison with others developing or present?[3]

A more complex diagnostic tool has been constructed by John Talbot (see following page). This chart can be used to help analyze problem areas within an organization by cross checking factors and their interrelationship in both the formal and informal structures.

PLAN FOR ACTION

Following such a process of clarification for diagnosis, a plan of action might follow. The earlier one can get to this stage, the better the opportunity to deal creatively with the conflict dynamics. Change inevitably follows conflict and our concern is that this be constructive change. Some factors that help lead to a constructive experience follow:

1. If conflict is arising from modification of established practice or organization, make certain that the need for modification has been clearly established.
2. Bring everyone affected by the change into the decision-making process.
3. Attempt to deal directly with emerging grievances as early as possible.
4. Keep long-range planning and goal setting out in front of any modification or change.
5. Encourage communication training throughout the congregation, alerting as many as possible to sensitivity of feelings and to nuances of meaning and perception.
6. Provide opportunities for common corporate experiences to deal with the possibility of divergent perceptions, allowing for theological reflection in the process.

M-C-P DIAGNOSTIC MATRIX
by John Talbot

Membership	—	Control	—	Product
M		C		P
(who)		(how)		(what)

people process — — — — — — — — — — — — — —

— — — — — — — — — — — — — — — — —work process

bridge — — — — — — — — — — — — *Formal Structure* — —

	P	Organ. GOALS Person.	P parent ROLES Event or pattern of acceptance — Ascribed behavior within organ.	YIELD Needs actively being met	*flow*
	C	STATUS Influence & power	POWER (Control) Organic or invested	STRUCTURE P Parent	
	M	INCLUSION (more members more power) must integrate new and old	NORMS	Formal news COMMUNI-CATION Gossip Grapevine	

Belonging for all

M	C	P

Informal Structure

Problem *Membership Factors:*	GOALS, STATUS, *INCLUSION,* NORMS, COMMUNICATION
Problem *Control Factors:*	*POWER,* STRUCTURE, ROLES, *STATUS,* NORMS
Problem *Product Factors:*	GOALS, ROLES, *YIELD,* STRUCTURE, COMMUNICATION

232

7. Be sure that dissident groups are represented in basic decision-making bodies in the church for the sake of communication and confrontation.
8. Keep a redemptive, accepting atmosphere throughout the congregation by such as Koinonia groups, or if necessary, a conciliator to help deal with key issues.
9. Foster negotiation and compromise where possible, especially allowing for factions to admit to their own intransigence after seeing more than one side as valid in an issue.[4]

Some conflicts may have gone beyond the state suggested above and require stronger action. Strategies for these more serious conflicts may be broadly dealt with as follows:

1. Try to remove the conflict from the win/lose context, allowing for a new image to develop that is inclusive in the final product.
2. Halt the expansion of the conflict and the persons involved. It helps to recognize the early signs and be preventative rather than fighting big fires.
3. Employ G.R.I.T. (graduated reciprocal reduction in tension). Each side gives a little at a time, recognizing the dangers of an uncontrolled conflagration.
4. Use bargaining and negotiating techniques employed in labor-management relations.
5. Work toward subordinate goals that all may buy into, and which just might leave the conflicting issues on the periphery.
6. Call in a mediator or referee, an external person without authority, that can help the various sides initiate the above strategies.

7. Use arbitration involving an external person with authority granted by all to resolve the conflicting issues.[5]

Skill Training

The discussion thus far may prompt this question: Where does one get the skills necessary to implement some of the suggestions given? Neither clergy nor lay leadership seem to possess this necessary training to help diagnosis and resolution of conflict. Some programs have been developed to meet this need. One such resource is offered by the United Methodist Church under the leadership of Charles P. Jaeger of the Board of Discipleship, called the "Utilizing Conflict Learning System." Trained leaders help persons in congregations to learn how to utilize conflict. The system consists of four three-hour learning modules that comprise the whole of the learning system. It is a twelve-hour total experience. The training consists of:

1. Experiencing the system as a learner
2. Participating in a coaching session to re-examine the system from the perspective of a leader and to receive leader's materials
3. Leading the system at least once, with an experienced leader serving as either co-leader or coach/observer

The four modules cover material on: 1) getting conflict in focus, 2) responding to conflict: choices, 3) enabling choices, 4) challenge to faithful encounter. Seven basic skills help to achieve these ends.

1. Help persons develop a personal power base in order to avoid insecure and depressive behavior.

2. Develop a solid base for relationship, which includes acceptance and trust.
3. Develop creative communications, which include in-depth listening and subjective responding.
4. Learn assumption filtering or reality testing.
5. Discover goal identification for the involved parties, working toward the establishing of overlapping of goals that leads to a win/win situation.
6. Select creative alternatives through such processes as brainstorming, selecting, and evaluating.
7. Establish contracts for acting on chosen alternatives.[6]

Even with the best of training and planning, disrupted expectations result in the need to enter into a planned renegotiation mode. The model uses the term "pincher" to describe these moments of disrupted expectations. If a pinch is experienced, planned renegotiation leads back to sharing of information and negotiating expectations again. This planned renegotiation model was designed by John J. Sherwood and included in the Jaeger training book.[7]

Relational Strategies

It is easy to move into a simplified problem-solving process when difficulties arise in groups and organizational life and to miss the locus of the problem. Intellectually, we can see the need to: 1) define the problem, 2) test the definition with full problem review, 3) develop alternatives, 4) debate alternatives, 5) test solution choice, 6) implement, 7) evaluate. This thorough-going, problem-solving process may well miss the source of the problem. As said before, the problem is not the problem, but the relationship. A task orientation is not sufficient to get at the source.

Relational strategies are needed also in order to effect a comprehensive problem-solving approach. Some suggestions for procedure may be as follows:

1. Help the parties to face and accept the complexity of the motivations of individuals and parties to the conflict. Do not oversimplify. This can be avoidance of the conflict to deny the complexities.
2. Humanize and reharmonize each party in the conflict situation. This is to accept the integrity and potential of each for growth and learning.
3. Internalize the conflict by bringing the claims of the opponents *objectively* together with your own and *feel* what is at stake on both sides.
4. Perceive the common goals and values inherent in the situation as relationships between parties are changed. Creative resolution requires change by all.
5. Accept conflict as natural and inherent such that it does not threaten. This will help to avoid strategies of denial or evasion.
6. Build and maintain a methodology to allow growth-releasing resolution to conflict whenever it appears.[8]

A process model which takes seriously the relational aspect of dealing with conflict is one developed by Blaine F. Hartford, Director of the Niagara Institute of Behavioral Science in Niagara, New York. The first part of the model deals with the relational aspect.

1. Attempt to clarify differences. Governing values can shift or can be doubted.
2. Review similarities or overlap of views. Try to find a consensus in standards for the relationship.

3. Share honest expression of feelings or reason for opposition. This is the serious attempt to remove personal blocks to the relationship.
4. Define interdependence (mutual goals, needs, and resources).
5. Check out the feeling tone for development of trust. If trust is present, proceed. If not, return to step one and start over.
6. Finally, define the problem as it is now perceived.
7. Look at alternative ways of getting at the problem.
8. Test the alternatives for feasibility.
9. Select an alternative to work on agreed to by all.
10. Implement it.
11. Evaluate by all after achieving some distance from the problem.

This process is based on the idea that change takes place in the people, not in the problem. The dynamics of this process are described by Hartford as: Conflict → Competition → Collaboration. If all energies can be utilized throughout the conflict such that they go toward enhancing the organization, then the organization can truly be said to be stronger as a result of having conflict. This is the possibility for the church as an organization of the Christian community to function to its potential.

Substantive Conflict

Decision making is a task function that we all must face in the church and other organizations. It has its various phases that must be worked through. Scheidel and Crowell have creatively developed two major phases to follow in decision making—a diverging phase and a converging phase.

The diverging phase is characterized by exploration, examination, and testing. It is the creative thinking process. The converging phase represents the comparison, evaluation, and choice stages. It is this latter process that is one of conflict. A group diverges as individuals (creative) and then must come back together (conflict) to work as a team for decision making.[9]

This creativity of the diverging phase is valuable. In order to get the most from it, take the following steps:

1. Be open to speculation. Have the courage to hear half-formed ideas with little apparent strength as of the present.
2. Keep wide open in the search. Hold off any restrictions at first.
3. Encourage ideas from *everyone*.
4. Give genuine appreciation to differences of ideas, views, terms, and interpretations.
5. Carefully hold back evaluation of any kind.[10]

The hostility and conflict will come at the juncture of the diverging and the converging phases. It can be described as the *storming* stage. From the intentional individual diverging, progress has to be made to bring the people into a task-oriented team for choice making. Consensus will be helped by paying attention to the following factors:

1. A *degree* of conflict is helpful when related to the task.
2. Facts and expert judgment do help resolve *substantive* conflict.
3. Orderly treatment of topics is helpful. Planned agenda with some flexibility helps.

4. Members should be helped to discuss *one* issue at a time. Get closure before moving on.
5. Members must understand what is being said. Use feedback to check understanding. Work on listening skills.
6. The chairperson should direct the seeking for information of an objective, factual nature. More solutions than usual should be offered in a tentative manner (strong leadership role).
7. When group members seem to like each other personally, substantive conflict is more easily resolved.[11]

Some further suggestions for handling conflict which will arise in this converging, decision-making phase are:

1. Manage and do not suppress the task conflict.
2. Keep the conflict on the task level and do not allow it to develop interpersonally. Do so by asking what it is that *all* desire, such as goals and underlying values. Keep all thinking together, openly, on task.
3. Increase the leader's central, direct role if task conflict intensifies. Neither parliamentary nor dictatorial style is helpful. A clear, understood plan of action is needed.
4. Increase the quality of listening done in the group to facilitate cooperative reasoning.
   a. Listen to *locate* the core of the difference.
   b. Listen to be able to *link* the new thought with the group thought line.
5. Facilitate the management by having the leader set the example for no rambling but rather clear statements.[12]

It may not be possible to keep all interaction at a task level during this converging process. It may be necessary to stop the intellectual activity and focus on the interpersonal prob-

lem causing disruptive, emotional stress. Do not try to diagnose the psychological whys of the stress, but rather rebuild
the feeling of group security and trust before trying to move
on with the task.[13] The leader must move with openness and
strength into the interpersonal problem to give security to
those involved. The group can and should be supportive to
each in conflict.

COMPLEX ORGANIZATIONS

Large churches can be very complex organizations. These
organizations need to pay particular attention to both their
structure *and* their process. The Likerts have developed a
model for complex organizations to help them deal creatively
with the potential for conflict. It is called a System 4 interaction-influence network. Reference has been made in prior
sections of this book to some helpful diagnoses and processes
that come out of a System 4 organization. I do not wish to
go into detail on this pattern here, but rather refer the reader
to their book again for more complete coverage.[14]

A procedural suggestion that can be entered here is the key
point in their structural design. It is called linked, multiple,
overlapping groups. A System 4 consists of cohesive work
groups with high performance goals linked together by persons who hold overlapping membership in two or more
groups. Problem solving is done in these cohesive, overlapping work groups by consensus. An essential function of the
link pins is to provide for information flow and to establish
reciprocal influence between the two groups of which the
person is a member. This helps to make sure that both groups
have the same statement of problems, the same facts and
knowledge of the situational requirements, the same awareness of differences and conflicts. The linking also assures that

the same pacing is kept by each group so that no group goes ahead and sets a solution before the others are ready and forces it upon them. The link pins mobilize the motivational forces and focus them on constructive problem solving. The focus is upon reaching resolution acceptable by all and making them operationally effective in a complex organization. Influence is exerted, with trust, in at least two different directions by the link pins such that communication flows responsibly for compatible solutions effectively for all. This coordination is essential for resolving conflicts constructively in large organizations. The linkages perform the needed strong bonding for the whole group fabric.[15]

With such structural assurance, sound intellectual problem solving can be used with more possibility for success. Procedures such as the following are suggested:

1. Locate the problem and focus it clearly. Be sure that it is the *real* problem.
2. Define the criteria which the solution must meet to be satisfactory. These are the essential ones. Then list those that are desirable also.
3. Search for all promising solutions. List them. Try to brainstorm in order to get different frames of reference or ways of looking at the problem to develop new and better solutions.
4. Obtain all relevant facts for the extent to which each solution would meet the criteria that are essential as well as the desirables.
5. Evaluate all suggested solutions in terms of the criteria and desirables.
6. Choose the solution which best meets the criteria. Eliminate first the solutions that don't meet the criteria of essential conditions. Then, eliminate progressively

those which meet desirable conditions least satisfactorily.

7. Check the solution finally selected against the problem as stated to be sure it really solves the problem. Check also for bad side effects.[16]

It must be remembered that the emotional factors present in any group are of great import and will affect any attempt at the above intellectual problem-solving approach. Basically, they distort the perception of the problem. Supportive relations must be maintained in order to make such procedures work.

Where there are bitter resentments that are a part of the conditions, a suggested plan follows.   It is assumed that influential persons are dissatisfied with the present situation.

1. The process of change of situation begins with the selection of a desired or ideal model.

2. Measure the key human organizational variables to see how close the present interaction-influence network approaches the desired model.

3. Analyze, interpret, and diagnose. Expert assistance may be needed here for data interpretation.

4. Plan the action based on step three. Use principles as follows:

   a. Focus on the causal variables which include leadership behavior and structure.

   b. Move toward a win/win style or System Four model slowly.

   c. Involve those whose behavior has to change to bring the desired improvements in planning the action to be taken.

  d. Use objective, impersonal evidence as much as possible in the action-planning process.

  e. Use integrative goals and mutual interests as much as possible in decision making.

  f. If possible, have those who are most powerful and influential take the initiative in improvement of the program.

  g. Conduct the action planning in supportive atmosphere. Training may be needed for action plans to be executed.

5. The action plans are put into operation. This improvement cycle should be reported each year for a few years afterwards. Remeasure the interaction-influence network. Build a highly effective network where conflict is likely.[17]

REFEREES

Some conflict just cannot find fruitful resolution without a third party. Leas and Kittlaus describe the process of choosing a referee for conflict resolution in their book, *Church Fights*.[18] The referee helps to organize the process in dealing with conflict situations. S/he could come from several constituencies. Such person may come from within the church's formal leadership or from its informal leadership. A referee may have to come from outside the church organization as an unknown, but professionally qualified.

Qualifications for a referee would include the following:

1. Substantive conflict is not taken personally because of high ego strength.

2. There is high tolerance for ambiguity, ambivalence, and frustration.

3. There is confidence in self as a manager and the person shares confidence that resolution can be found in the conflict.
4. S/he is not an advocate for any particular solution, nor are sides allowed for the referee in the issues.
5. S/he has credibility with all sides.
6. The referee should be able to model behavior to participants.

Some assumptions for referees to operate under are the following, listed by Leas and Kittlaus:

1. Conflict is inevitable and resolvable.
2. Conformity is not required.
3. Few situations are hopeless.
4. One part affects another—reflecting a systems approach.
5. Each side probably has a piece of the truth.
6. There is some similarity between opponents—in both weaknesses and strengths.
7. The present problems are the ones to solve—focus on the NOW.
8. The process is of great importance as distinguished from the content.
9. There is no right answer.[19]

These assumptions come out of the experience that Leas and Kittlaus have had as referees. Such awareness helps the referee to establish rules to work with and to enforce those rules of operation for successful resolution. Resources are usually present within a congregation that can be developed to function as a neutral force in the management process. It is the referee's job to develop this potential.

Some skills for refereeing are necessary. They may be generally described as follows:

1. Familiarity with research data and concepts of persons and groups in conflict.
2. Experience with group dynamics.
3. Work in disciplined reflection with groups.[20]

There is risk involved in the decision to go with a referee. Such persons may reach conclusions for themselves as to the right answer and push for such conclusion in the process. Or the referee may have such personal needs for inclusion and affection that s/he will not be able to keep control and give a very unsatisfied personal feeling to the deliberations. The referee can then easily become the scapegoat for the various parties.

The minister may well not be the best choice for a referee. Many see themselves as reconcilors and wish to perform as such in church fights. However, such image may carry with it the need to keep peace and not to open the conflict sufficiently for effective resolution. Usually, the minister is associated with a side in the conflict, true or not, and loses thereby any credibility for the referee role. In other words, the minister may well be part of the problem.[21]

Leas and Kittlaus provide a helpful outline for following the process of options in conflict management. A chart diagrams the various options of choice to move with or without a referee in facing conflict. The chart follows on the succeeding page (Chart 1).[22] It acts as a diagram of movement options to get a feel for the whole picture of managing a conflict in the church. Their book fills in the gaps.

A somewhat simplified model for working at conflict resolution was designed by A. M. Levi and G. Benjamin. Theirs is

Chart I. OPTIONS IN CONFLICT MANAGEMENT

By Leas and Kittlaus

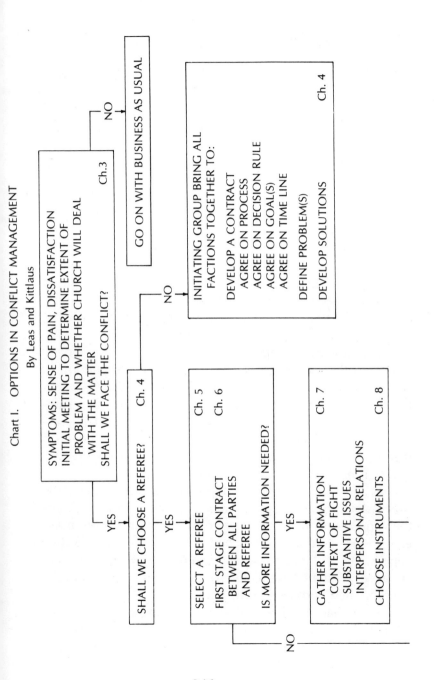

SYMPTOMS: SENSE OF PAIN, DISSATISFACTION
INITIAL MEETING TO DETERMINE EXTENT OF
PROBLEM AND WHETHER CHURCH WILL DEAL
WITH THE MATTER
SHALL WE FACE THE CONFLICT?   Ch.3

NO → GO ON WITH BUSINESS AS USUAL

YES

SHALL WE CHOOSE A REFEREE?   Ch. 4

NO → INITIATING GROUP BRING ALL
FACTIONS TOGETHER TO:

DEVELOP A CONTRACT
AGREE ON PROCESS
AGREE ON DECISION RULE
AGREE ON GOAL(S)
AGREE ON TIME LINE

DEFINE PROBLEM(S)

DEVELOP SOLUTIONS   Ch. 4

YES

SELECT A REFEREE   Ch. 5

FIRST STAGE CONTRACT   Ch. 6
BETWEEN ALL PARTIES
AND REFEREE

IS MORE INFORMATION NEEDED?

YES

GATHER INFORMATION   Ch. 7
CONTEXT OF FIGHT
SUBSTANTIVE ISSUES
INTERPERSONAL RELATIONS

CHOOSE INSTRUMENTS   Ch. 8

NO

246

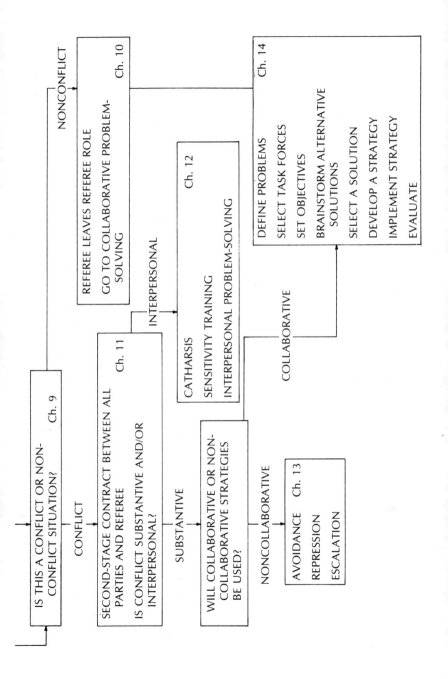

IS THIS A CONFLICT OR NON-CONFLICT SITUATION? · Ch. 9

CONFLICT

NONCONFLICT

SECOND-STAGE CONTRACT BETWEEN ALL PARTIES AND REFEREE   Ch. 11

IS CONFLICT SUBSTANTIVE AND/OR INTERPERSONAL?

REFEREE LEAVES REFEREE ROLE

GO TO COLLABORATIVE PROBLEM-SOLVING   Ch. 10

INTERPERSONAL

SUBSTANTIVE

CATHARSIS   Ch. 12

SENSITIVITY TRAINING

INTERPERSONAL PROBLEM-SOLVING

WILL COLLABORATIVE OR NON-COLLABORATIVE STRATEGIES BE USED?

NONCOLLABORATIVE

COLLABORATIVE

AVOIDANCE   Ch. 13

REPRESSION

ESCALATION

DEFINE PROBLEMS   Ch. 14

SELECT TASK FORCES

SET OBJECTIVES

BRAINSTORM ALTERNATIVE SOLUTIONS

SELECT A SOLUTION

DEVELOP A STRATEGY

IMPLEMENT STRATEGY

EVALUATE

247

a task model that utilizes the benefit of a consultant or referee. They developed this procedure out of a Jew and Arab rehearsal of Geneva.[23] The surprising degree of success with this model is attributed to the structured task format in contrast to process-oriented models. The task is led by consultants or referees with the participants giving content only. The diagram follows.

THE USE OF EXERCISES

Non-verbal exercises provide a ready resource for learning throughout the church. They are a valuable asset for groups, helping them to deal with dynamics that are difficult to talk about but can be experienced in a game or exercise setting with rules for control. Having common experience of some conflict dynamics, a group can get into a reflection on the event and begin to make integration with where they are in the group or organization of the church. This affective experience allows for the confronting of conflict under controls which reduce some of the fears associated with conflict. With sensitive timing and leadership, a pastor or lay person may use an exercise to work through a block in an organization's process.

An example of this potential is the use of the Fingertip Exercise on Power. Directions for the exercise are very simple. There should be no talking. Circles of from six to nine people are formed. Each person in the circle puts out his/her arms to each side and touches the fingertips of the person on either side. That fingertip contact must be maintained throughout the exercise. The action direction is merely to *experiment* with their own power. The results of group action are usually an immediate pressing off against the person on either side. It is a power play of forces to establish space and dom-

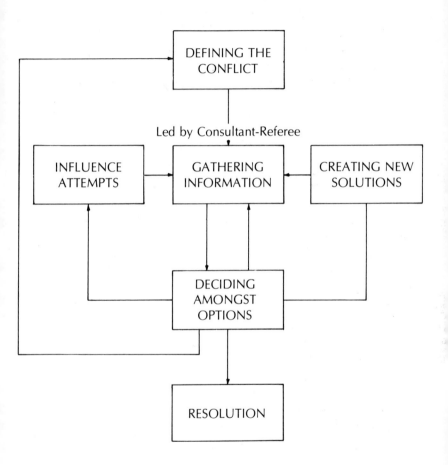

Chart 2.   A TASK MODEL
by Levi and Benjamin

inance over another. After some time at the win/lose game, persons will then experiment with another form of power-leadership. They will try to draw the group one way or another, establishing power of leadership. Power to thwart leadership may also be experienced by holding back movement or by actually sitting down, forcing a physical blockage to group progress. Possibly, the group could progress to a sense of community in which each comes together as one to dance or play.

Discussion of individual competitiveness and need for space and worth follows such an exercise, with easy reference to individual and group behavior within the organization. Problems of leadership relate to the individual's need for space and power, showing the differences between competitive win/lose behavior and a cooperative, consensus-producing experience both in the exercise and in the group's organizational life. It is possible to use such an exercise in the midst of a group's internal strife to get out the dynamics and to talk more freely about them. Personal space, equilibrium in the group, and personal worth all flow from the Fingertip Exercise on Power and can vitally affect a group in the throes of their organizational interpersonal conflict.

Other exercises can be used in similar ways. A more elementary exercise by which to start a group in their self-analysis is called Cross the Line. Pair up the people in dyads, standing facing each other across an imaginary line. This is a verbal exercise. The directions are to get the other person to cross over the line. Suggestions like the use of coercion, manipulation, or persuasion may be made for their thought and choice. Discussion following this exercise leads to the distinction between the win/lose and the win/win style of approach. Many will discover that their expectations set the stage for their actions. The simplest response to the dilemma of the exercise is to invite the person on the other side of the line to cross over to your side as you cross over to theirs, making each a "winner" and none a "loser." Usually, a variety of coercion, manipulation, or persuasion will be used by the participants. The discussion can well move to expectations or predilections for win/lose in our lifestyle or a cooperative, win/win style, and why we adopt that style. Psycho-theological understandings can come from such simple exercise experience. The person usually experiences a much more effective lesson this way than from an introductory lecture on the theory or morality of conflict.

Many exercises are available to help this educative process. They can be used in workshop format or judiciously timed and introduced in a regular meeting.

Procedures for dealing with conflict experienced in the church have been summarized in this chapter with the intent and understanding that clergy and lay leadership have sufficient training in their own professional and lay preparation to understand and to lead in their use. This may be a logical expectation and yet unreal. Training workshops or continuing education may be needed by such church leadership in order to deal adequately with this leadership expectation. Seminaries, colleges and universities, or management workshops provide such educational opportunities.

Notes

1. Rolla Swanson, "Planning Change and Dealing with Conflict: A Field Theory Model with Eleven Steps to Change," *Chicago Theological Seminary Register* 59, no. 4 (May 1969): 23.

2. Ibid., p. 26.

3. Charles A. Dailey, "The Management of Conflict," *Chicago Theological Seminary Register* 59, no. 4 (May 1969): 6.

4. Swanson, "Planning Change and Dealing with Conflict: A Field Theory Model with Eleven Steps to Change," p. 31.

5. Charles A. Dailey, "Reflections on the Elmhurst Case," *Chicago Theological Seminary Register* 59, no. 4 (May 1969): 15–16.

6. Charles P. Jaeger, ed., *Utilizing Conflict: A Learning System* (Nashville: Discipleship Resources, 1976), pp. 51–56.

7. Ibid., p. 61.

8. Robert R. Blake, Herbert A. Shepherd, and Jane S. Mouton, *Managing Intergroup Conflict in Industry* (Houston, Tex.: Gulf Publications Co., 1964), pp. 90ff.

9. Thomas Scheidel and Laura Crowell, *Discussing and Deciding: A Desk Book for Group Leaders and Members* (New York: Macmillan, 1979), pp. 162–165.

10. Ibid., p. 171.

11. Ibid., p. 204.

12. Ibid., pp. 221–225.

13. Ibid., p. 235.

14. Rensis and Jane Likert, *New Ways of Managing Conflict* (New York: McGraw-Hill, 1976).

15. Ibid., pp. 183–200.

16. Ibid., p. 126.

17. Ibid., pp. 308–312.

18. Speed Leas and Paul Kittlaus, *Church Fights: Managing Conflict in the Local Church* (Philadelphia: Westminster Press, 1973), pp. 60–76.

19. Ibid., pp. 67–72.

20. Ibid., p. 75.

21. Ibid., p. 74.

22. Ibid., pp. 52–53. Reproduced by permission.

23. A. M. Levi and A. Benjamin, "Jews and Arabs Rehearse Geneva: A Model of Conflict Resolution," *Human Relations* 20, no. 11 (November 1976): 1035–1044.

13 Specific Procedures for Using Creative Conflict in Religious Education

It was posited in our section on general considerations that the interpretive process was the center of the subject matter of religious education. The text and the interpreter must come to an understanding between the life situation of the text and the life situation of the interpreter. This stands not only for the student but also for the teacher. The essence of the dynamics of this interpretive process becomes the dynamics of listening and appropriating. Why is this important to conflicts in regard to religious education? The answer becomes obvious when you see the presuppositions and life situations that vary amongst the interpreters as well as their understanding of the life situation of the text. The variations of life situations present obvious conflict. The dialog then becomes most important as these presuppositions and basic life situations come to the fore and both student and teacher are afforded the opportunity for greater understanding of self, other, and text.

Since the emphasis here is on process, we are reminded again of our need to integrate the affective and cognitive elements in our religious education. This is a process which is not limited to childhood education, but to the full line of

253

education in the church. We face the ongoing need of all individuals in the church to interpret meaning and continually work on achieving new self-understanding in their faithing process. This again points us to the need to deal with conflict as we move through the growth process. The conflict involved in the developmental understanding of education occurs not only in the preoperational child who is dealing with the contradiction of his or her perception and thought process, but also the chronological adult who is dealing with changes of self-perception as s/he moves through the various stages of adulthood. Disequilibrium and movement toward restructuring are a part of the educational process of all ages. Conflict is at the center of this process.

This inherent conflict can be utilized intentionally in our church schools and other educational programs of the church. An instructional model referred to earlier under General Considerations can utilize the inducing of conflict in order to enhance movement from one developmental stage to another. Again, this is not limited to childhood, but also involves adult education. This places a heavy burden upon the instructor to be aware of the stage development of the student and to be able to develop intentional conflict that will aid the student in his/her developmental movement. One needs knowledge of the individual as well as mastery of the content. The lesson planning would need to reflect the confluent process, or the effective bringing together of cognitive and affective elements, in all of its complexity and personalization. The whole scope of values clarification serves as a helpful technique in completing the function just described.

The enhancement of self-awareness and self-understanding in the process of interpreting and finding meaning in life requires patience and intelligent strategizing. It appears much more difficult than the popular process of merely "giving the word," coming from conservative churches. I see this as a critical factor as we try to understand our present-day needs in religious development and self-understanding in the church. A popular demand exists for someone to give "the word" with authority. The condition of lower tolerance for ambiguity goes with that demand, making conflict most difficult to deal with. It seems that church persons today would much rather have someone tell them what to believe than to work it through for themselves. The need for security forces persons to respond to every little bit of authority which can be found in religious institutions. Cults grow fast under these conditions. Charismatic leaders draw tremendous support, but the developmental growth to which we have referred is not served by this need adaption. What can be done by one in religious education who wishes to plan for long-lasting, individually tested religious growth?

A MODEL OF CREATIVE CONFLICT

A specific model has been suggested by Dr. Robert L. Conrad from his unpublished dissertation at Princeton Theological Seminary. Dr. Conrad has shared a model which I think is a creative one, responding to the very theory and needs just previously described.[1] Conrad uses a learning process drawn from Luther's own personal growth and religious development correlated with a social-psychological process of Arthur Koestler from his book, *The Act of Creation* (New York: Macmillan Co., 1964). A dynamic of four steps emerge. Those four steps are: active struggle, passive resignation, unexpected insight, and long-range interpretation. These steps are more simply referred to as conflict, resignation, insight, and interpretation.[2] How am I, the teacher, to integrate these dynamic steps into a teaching model? The following are some steps that could be taken, as suggested by Conrad.

Teacher preparation:

1. Determine a conflict appropriate to the life of the learners.
   a. The conflict must be stated in terms of simultaneously opposing forces.
   b. The conflict must have the characteristic of universality.
   c. The conflict must be significant enough to engage the totality of the learner and lead to a "blocked situation."
2. Examine the opposing forces in the conflict, determining the way in which they show themselves in life. This aids in forming the questions to be asked in the group discussion on the conflict.
3. Select a medium that incorporates the conflict chosen. It can be a story, symbol, film, record, whatever.
4. Determine questions that can be asked in order to help the learner become aware of the conflicting forces involved.

After these four preparatory steps, the following would initiate the teaching/learning session:

Conflict Phase

1. Present the conflict medium.
2. Present the questions related to the conflict incorporated in the medium.

3. Pull forth the learner's own statement of the conflict as s/he understands it.
4. Explore the conflict as experienced in the learners' lives. Questions are involved here to sharpen the conflict so that it might be felt as deeply and sharply as possible.

Resignation Phase

1. Allow the learner to break off dealing with the conflict—possible use of silence or other activity.

Insight Phase

1. Allow for as much openness as possible so that the learner may experience a revelation of God as one who forgives, accepts, and frees a person. This is a stage of risk over which the teacher, group, or individual has little control.

Interpretation Phase

1. Provide a context in which insights can be shared, interpreted, and verified as constructive resolutions to the conflict.
2. Allow for the possibility of interpersonal help in the testing of validity and insights.[3]

This particular model of the use of creative conflict in religious education might be generally described as a "personal source model" which has as its goal the growth in creativity and insight.

WEEKEND LEARNING LAB FOR YOUTH

The youth age group brings a particular need to deal with conflict in the midst of their educational experience. The personality development of youth centers on the inner conflict of dependence/independence. This has been discussed earlier in the prior section of this book. Their needs are quite strong for the affective dimensions of education and relationships. It has been found that youth respond more affectively, or emotionally, to conflict events of tension, frustration, and aggression than do older persons—a finding cited earlier in this book, one based on a study by the Committee on Adolescence of the Group for the Advancement of Psychiatry, in *Normal Adolescence* (New York: Scribner's, 1968). The chapter on affective education mentioned our need to be interested in persons with their feeling, their doing and acting, as much as with their thinking. This is particularly true with youth.

Generally speaking, creative conflict in education is badly needed to develop interpersonal competence in relating to other human beings. This pertains to all levels, but it fits especially for the age group of youth. Their intrapersonal conflict between aggressive impulses and socially sanctioned moral norms of behavior leads to the projection of aggression onto others. This develops into interpersonal sources of conflict. Discrepancy in power relations between persons, usually with adults, becomes evident. Competition is often most keen as a source of interpersonal conflict. Youth often express it in the midst of classroom activity. Therefore, special attention needs to be brought to the development of classroom activity with youth, including confrontive/supportive activity that allows for expression of conflict, yet maintains affective support for the experience.

One way of working with youth in the church makes use of

the weekend learning lab. When dealing with conflict, it is most often advantageous to have longer periods of time at your disposal in order to work through the dynamics that arise. A weekend learning lab meets this need. A good way to approach such a lab utilizes the conflicts already present in a youth group in order to learn the nature of conflict and strategies for healing. Conflict arises both within the individual and between individuals, and there are various ways to utilize this conflict.

One way might be to incorporate the obvious conflict between youth and adults by bringing in formal leaders and others to be a part of a learning lab experience. Some of the issues of the generation gap may then be explored with youth getting out their feelings of confinement and alienation, and adults getting out their feelings about values they have held but youth do not.

A second approach to a weekend lab could be the combining of the youth groups from two or more local churches that gather together such obvious divisions as white-black or Anglo-Hispanic, and build in the source of conflict to be dealt with in the lab. Of course, all such carefully planned conflict also needs a commitment to a community which will reach out and heal.

A third possibility for a lab merely focuses on the group itself and its members who know each other and have a continuing relationship. Conflicts always lie beneath the surface and are rarely dealt with in such groups. The weekend may be used to expose those conflicts and begin the process of dealing with them directly.

I would like to suggest a plan which surfaces the conflicts present in the youth group as subject matter for the weekend. Four sessions are suggested—each of about one and a half to two hours long—which could guide a weekend program.[4]

Session One

Using the whole group, gather impressions of what the unit might be about entitled "The Christian Uses of Conflict." The unit may be ordered from the Graded Press, 1969, Methodist Publishing House, Nashville, Tennessee. Allow for a variety of definitions. After attempts at definition, the booklet should be introduced. This would include identification of issues and topics with a brief synopsis. Other resources could be displayed on a table and time allowed following the booklet introduction to browse through those gathered resources.

Session Two

The identification of real or fanciful divisions of your particular group may be introduced. Separate small groups could be formed to allow this identification to take on particular meanings for the members. Each small group should list those divisions within the group of which they are aware. Further breakdown might be made between more important and less important factors. These small groups could then report back to the whole with some identification and clarification of their listed divisions. After reporting back, the small groups should be formed again to attempt closer identification of the actual conflicts that are present in their group. This merely identifies and does not solve the conflicts. The values which are at stake should be listed by both sides of the conflicts identified. If this process proves too difficult for the group, an audio-visual on conflict could be introduced.

If the group seems ready to move into the identified conflicts, the gathering of the whole might begin negotiation by some role playing using the values that have been isolated.

Session Three

Continue the role-playing negotiation. Particular observers should be designated for reporting back. These observers could ask themselves such questions as: Where did the negotiators come out? Was there resolution or breakdown? Why? Were values sacrificed? How did the collaboration come about? If it did not, why not? How could the negotiators have done better? What were the major tactics used by the negotiators? Were they valid or invalid? The various conflicts that have been isolated may be brought up one at a time.

Following the local group conflict resolution, the relating of their conflicts to the larger conflicts of the "outside world" could begin. What kind of negotiations would be necessary to resolve the larger conflicts in the larger society?

Session Four

By now, one of three conditions may be realized. 1) Real conflicts have broken out and are absorbing all energy. 2) Real conflicts stayed hidden and role playing has been polite, getting nowhere. 3) Real conflict has become ambiguously visible. Focus for this session should be upon seeking the realities of the group conflict and working at more honest negotiation. Small groups might be formed in order to evaluate and report back to the larger group. Another audio-visual on conflict might be utilized as a means of helping total perspective.

Plans should be made at this point to continue the gains from this weekend and plan into forthcoming activities.

A closing celebration should be designed as a means of affirming the values of the larger Christian community and the loving, supporting base of their own community.

Future programming ideas could well come from such a lab weekend. Group conflicts could point to the needs of individual members. Conflict could be noticed in parallel between the youth group and the larger church. These conflicts of Christian community may become the focus for other planning. The individual focus may emerge as a place for more work. How does a person find himself/herself in conflict and how may s/he learn new modes of dealing with his/her individual conflict? The result of these experiences should prove to strengthen the participants. A strong sense of Christian community should emerge. Self-identity and self-worth should also grow. The whole support nature of the group could be strengthened by this type of experience. A gain in trust should be a major product.

A TEACHING RHYTHM WITH VERBAL AND NON-VERBAL EXERCISES

A weekend lab or a classroom has a particular rhythm according to the way in which one teaches. I am convinced that the use of verbal or non-verbal communication exercises plays an important part in the type of learning situation which is most effective in attempting to utilize conflict. Conflict cannot escape from being an emotional experience. The affective dimension becomes most important.

In my own teaching of conflict management and utilization, I have found a particular rhythm that has been most beneficial. That rhythm begins with the introduction of theoretical material on the cognitive level. Ideas are presented and concepts explained, with as much illustrative material as possible in order to help create understanding. Identification with the theoretical materials is pursued as much as possible.

VERBAL AND NON-VERBAL EXERCISES

Following the presentation of theoretical material or ideas, I bring in the affective dimensions with the use of verbal or non-verbal exercises. Exercises (as an educative tool) have produced a mixed reaction amongst teachers and leaders of groups. My experience is that the verbal or non-verbal exercise makes a valuable tool in learning about self and conflict.

Research on the value of structured exercises for learning shows inconclusive evidence. However, some evidence from research corroborates my own teaching experience. For instance, high exercise type groups produce a high feeling of group closeness, cohesiveness, or sense of community over low exercise type groups.[5] This experience has a positive benefit toward learning in the group because of the establishment of trust and a higher degree of self-worth and self-esteem, which is critical in the movement toward constructive experience with conflict.

Research also shows that high exercise groups show increased self-understanding, compared with low exercise groups.[6] Self-understanding is vital to the establishing of constructive conflict over against the use of conflict as a way of working off emotional backlog from previous experiences.

Related to self-understanding, exercises afford the participant the opportunity to experiment with new behavior.[7] Participants can begin to allay the fears of conflict as a dynamic in their lives. Fear of conflict is a basic force in creating the flight syndrome. In times of uncertainty, opportunity to try out new behavior becomes a valuable tool for survival and learning. The mainline churches of Protestantism have had to face major conflict within because of their inability or desire not to give responses to those who want simple answers in this present "correct answer syndrome" running through the churches. The more evangelical churches, which are giving out simple and quick answers, are growing mightily for that very reason. Ambiguity is difficult to tolerate and creates the base for intrapersonal and then interpersonal and intergroup conflict in our churches and in society.

High exercise group participants see their group experience as more constructive than those with low exercise experience.[8] They feel like they learned more, although over time this feeling tends to level out.

Overall evaluation of high exercise groups over low exercise groups remains mixed. It seems that other factors have considerable influence over outcomes, such as factors of group climate and leader strategy.[9] My experience indicates that group climate is aided greatly by the use of structured exercises. Trust and self-esteem grow as a result for both individual and group.

What are some of these exercises that give valuable assistance to persons struggling to deal with conflict? How might they be used in the organizations of the church? Structured groups for education in the church, adult or children and youth, provide a good setting for the use of structured exercises. However, as noted earlier in this book, exercises can be used in a task group in order for the participants to get some needed understanding of what is blocking their task progress as a result of conflict experienced.

The exercise provides an opportunity to work on the ideas or concepts shared at the beginning of the educative rhythm projected earlier. Experiential learning integrates the cognitive and the affective dimensions. It brings the ideas into an identity with the self and the self's experiences. Experiential learning also makes use of others who shared the experiences as they give feedback to each other and share their insights and perceptions from the exercise. Self-awareness and awareness of others have been referred to earlier as critical to the positive appropriation of the conflict experience.

Some particularly valuable exercises for use have been suggested by Arthur L. Foster in his article on conflict in the *Chicago Theological Seminary Register*.[10] Trust building is a primary goal for exploring conflict dynamics. Foster makes various suggestions on how to experience trust with one another in a group. If the conflict is between youth and parents, begin with a blind walk or trust walk. The youth leads the parent to experience the world without sight and to heighten touch, taste, smell, and hearing. Leading each other alternately by the hand through the surrounding environment can provide a fruitful base for later exploration between parents and youth. The trust factor is the important beginning point which each must experience.

Another possible beginning point for exploring conflict dynamics could be the eyecologue. This exercise begins with people divided into dyads and asked to be silent and to look directly into the eyes of the other. Usually, silence is most difficult to achieve because of the nervous laughter or talking. Being known and knowing can cause anxiety, and can involve too much intimacy to handle. This forms the basis for discussion on this important dynamic of conflict. Husbands and wives can do this exercise with real benefit for their marriage relationship.

While still working on building trust, a game can be helpful which starts with either pairing or breaking into small groups. The directions are to have the people stand in the center of the circle or with their back to a partner, close their eyes, and let themselves fall stiff-legged into the arms of the partner or outer ring of the closed circle. Allow each person to have the experience and then talk about the feelings of trust or mistrust and the sense of responsibility felt by the receivers.

After some basic trust develops, other exercises help a group get into conflict dynamics. A group may have participants who feel they have been boxed out or boxed in as an individual either in the current group or at some other time. This provides for feelings which emerge in conflicting/tense relationships through other matters. This situation can be worked out by two different exercises. One called Break In has individuals volunteering to experience the "left out" feelings by standing outside a circle formed by the other participants. The circle locks arms and forms a barrier to be broken. The outside person tries all methods to "get in." The other matched exercise is called Break Out. This time, a person volunteers to act out the feelings of being trapped into an image or role that he/her does not like. The volunteer is on the inside of the circle and the circle of participants tries to keep him/her in. Escaping the trap and feeling responsibility for keeping one in a trap provide good data to discuss how conflict is generated from this common phenomenon.

Sometimes it becomes helpful to merely act out the frustration of conflict. A simple game of arm wrestling provides for energy release from the aggressive feelings and reduces mere verbal warfare in groups or may actually call it forth to be dealt with.

Another good beginning to get people into their conflict dynamics is to use the Conflict Self-Portrait. Self understanding can emerge from responding to the following open ended questions:

1. When I am in a conflict situation, I . . . ?
2. When I am in a conflict situation, I feel . . . ?
3. I resolve my conflict by. . . .
4. In conflict situations, I would like to. . . .

After each person fills out the answers (which can either have suggested answer choices or not), all are invited to form groups around the collated responses to each question, one question at a time. They talk about why they responded that way, what other responses they would like to have made, and why they did not make that response.

This exercise provides for some self-analysis and openness to individual emotions which are shared and explored with one another. Trust building prior to this particular experience facilitates confidence among the members and reduces inhibitions to self-understanding and expression.

Another exercise accomplishing much the same goals is one which utilizes Virginia Satir's theory on conflict and congruency. The whole group or each group subdivision is asked to try out four actions which are ways of dealing with conflict between self and another. The first tactic for conflict resolve is to try placating or blocking out the self as a person of worth to accommodate the other's demands. Try it out and tune into the feelings that are produced as a result. Then second, try the experience of blaming the other for the problem, which blocks out the other person as an individual of worth and value. Third, experience or role play the use of a "correct and reasonable approach," which gives the feeling of blocking out both the self and the other person as being of value, worth, and feeling. Finally, try treating the conflict as irrelevant and of no consequence—thus blocking out self, other, and even the context of the conflict.[11]

The opportunity to try out these varied responses to conflict forces each person to assess his/her natural responses and to decide on their relative merits. A fuller understanding and awareness of what the various responses to conflict imply influences future choices and decision making.

CONFLICT MINI-LAB

Another line of exercises referred to earlier allows individuals in a group to open up conflict dynamics for themselves. These exercises could follow introductory statements or theory about the nature of conflict for further personal understanding and integration. To begin with, an exercise called Cross the Line opens up the individual's comfort with various strategies for solving a simple conflict. The directions for this exercise are found on p. 250 of the preceding chapter. The experience sought here is an alternative to a win/lose strategy in conflict, or to see a possible win/win strategy. The effects of an adversary relationship versus a cooperative one can come forth out of this simple exercise. These are basic learnings to understand and to experience if one desires to move toward conflict utilization in the church as an organization.

The follow-up to an exercise like Cross the Line might be one termed the Fingertip Exercise on Power. Here, power is introduced as a basic phenomenon in understanding conflict dynamics, providing opportunity to experiment with an individual's sense of personal power. Directions for this exercise are found on p. 248 of the preceding chapter. The need for personal space is dramatically exhibited as participants push off against each other, experimenting with their power. Power of leadership and followership can be experienced in this exercise also, usually after space has been established. Self understanding and group understanding follows easily from a debriefing of this exercise. The dynamics of conflict become more than words and some of the participants' experiences of conflict may well become better understood, aiding future conflict resolution.

An exercise to continue this line of experiences is one called Win-As-Much-As-You-Can.[12] Here, conflict dynamics become more intense. Large groups need to be paired and situated in a square like a square dance set. A scoring sheet plus interpretation is shared with each pair in each square.

The ten rounds of play create increasing tension and test of trust and manipulation skills. The interpretation of the title of the exercise will determine direction and experience of play. Each paired team must determine each round whether they will choose to write down an X or a Y, with the understanding of how the various combinations in their square will determine the score for each on that round. Cooperative versus competitive dynamics are tested with this exercise. Discussion that follows can be very fruitful in understanding how conflict develops and escalates, how to deal with it in an interdependent group situation, and the impact on individuals. The importance of trust and cooperative attitudes versus competitive ones surface as central through this exercise.

Moving deeper into experience of conflict through group exercises, I recommend the use of a simulation game called Star Power.[13] A larger group needs to be divided into three different groups. These are named the circles, the squares, and the triangles. Conflict is built into the dynamics of this game by the distribution and the exchange of chips. A "fixed" distribution forces frustration and competition for power, stimulating conflict dynamics with potentially explosive power. Limited movement between groups is regulated by the scoring procedure which builds into power and control by a select group. The value with this exercise emanates from the frustration and control by others, or by oneself, and afterward reviewing ones feelings and actions. Increased self-knowledge and integration with earlier theoretical input are the rewards of this exercise.

An even more intense experience of conflict can come from a simulation called Powerplay by George Peabody and Paul Dietterich.[14] This exercise in conflict deals with the subjects of collaboration, negotiation, and coercion. It takes a longer period of time to play than the preceding exercises. The use of power comes out centrally in focus, allowing the player to experience the development of power in self and others and to make decisions and actions on the basis of that power. Important debriefing structure is included in this simulation. A good bibliography also follows the play section of the participant's manual.

PERCEPTION

The experience of confronting varied perceptions of the same thing helps people to understand conflict dynamics. As a part of these exercises, varied perceptions of the same situation show conflict sources. A simple teaching exercise that shows our limitations in perception and how we can fall prey to conflict from our limitations is one based on a series of nine dots. The situation is as follows:

• • •
• • •
• • •

Instructions are to connect these nine dots with four interconnected straight lines such that a line goes through each dot, without raising your marker from the paper. Boxed in expectations of a square prohibit most from seeing the possibilities of completing according to direction. The need to be open to new perceptions beyond your own past experience becomes clear when the completed puzzle comes out like the following:

Other perception exercises are also available to aid in the understanding of how differing perceptions of the same ex-

perience or information can precipitate conflict.[15] A favorite
of mine is one called "The Young or Old Lady." It is found in
the same reference as the nine dots—the work of Napier and
Gershenfeld. A drawing of a lady can be perceived as either
an old figure or a young one, depending on the eye's focus.
To be able to see both is an enlightening experience as a
person grows toward consensus building and collaboration.

VALUES EXERCISES

Values games are another source of experience in which
conflict dynamics may be probed. Those most helpful are the
ones based on working at a consensus for resolution of a
conflict. In a book called *Values Clarification* by Simon,
Howe, and Kirschenbaum, there are a number of possibilities
for use.[16] Consensus building does not allow for conflict of
values to be solved by a simple majority vote, as is most often
done in our churches. Here, you must work through the differences of values for understanding each other and the establishment of group values. An exercise like Alligator River,
which may be found in the above book, makes the experience both a fun time as well as a real live test. Reflection and
discussion bring forth learnings that help in self-understanding and the appreciating of the other's positions or values.
A simple introductory exercise which can help each person
get into appreciation of the other's values is called Values
Focus. It can be found in the Simon book also.

These exercises described always provide experiences to
work through deeper feelings or to try new behavior to meet
conflicting emotions. The experiences are then related to the
theory presented earlier for internalization and integration
with individual life learnings. This attempts to move the education out of a "head trip" into life-integrated learning. Conflict education in particular needs the help of movement from

intellectualization to life relevance with verbal sharing of feelings which are difficult to express. Psychic meanings get expressed into physical actions for the breaking of an impasse or block to conscious dealing with the internal condition. Conflict must be brought to consciousness as a beginning step for resolution. That consciousness also needs help to find verbal expression. Exercises can become that valuable tool for accomplishing these aims.

DEBRIEFING

The presentation of the theory or intellectual material about conflict needs balancing by the experiential. This enlivening of the theory is not yet sufficient. The reflection-discussion of the experience finally draws forth the necessary full comprehension. The process finds completion when the individual reflects and learns from self and others. This is called "debriefing." The exercises can provide the opportunity to try new behavior as well as learn about established patterns. Both the older patterns and the new behavior need this reflection in order to help the person decide which is better or at least to become more aware of why such behavior is used.

Feedback provides a helpful process to be used in a group which has experienced conflict and attempted various means to its resolve. Feedback is a sharing of a perception of an individual's behavior or an assessment of a response in order to help that person see the impact that behavior has on others. It helps a person evaluate the effectiveness of that behavior and may lead to a decision to change in the future. Criteria for giving feedback include the following:

1. A willingness to receive feedback by the person(s) within the group doing debriefing.

2. An understanding by all in the feedback process that there are needs present in both the giver and the receiver of the feedback, and that the focus should be centered on the receiver's needs.
3. A focus on specific behavior and its effects rather than sweeping generalizations.
4. Non-judgmental or descriptive comments which reduce the need for defensive comebacks and allow for optimum appropriation of the feedback.
5. Focus on workable goals that are both important enough to expend the energy on as well as feasible enough to lead people to expect success.

The intent of the feedback process in the rhythm for teaching-learning presented here is to help to integrate the cognitive theory and the personal experience in the exercises in a way that leads to change or learning. Change or learning is in itself a conflict. Do I want to change, or not?? Am I satisfied to remain with my current behavior patterns and values? What effects will either choice have for me and for others? Resolution of such personal growth conflict may bring in many of the dynamics of conflict resolution that have been introduced in this book.

CONCLUSION

The rhythm of theory presentation, experiential exercises (verbal and non-verbal), and debriefing is a style which can be used in adult education or in the religious education of children and youth as long as they are at the stage of conceptual learning. Curriculum can be written in this format, or the format can be drawn from an established curriculum. Nonetheless, conflict can be either the subject matter for learning or the process by which learning on any subject takes place. An understanding of conflict is necessary for either. This book attempts to give that understanding for those who are responsible for learning throughout the church. Learning does not have to be in a classroom to be considered education. The whole church and its activities provide the locus. Reference has been made to the regular educational channels of religious education in the classroom of church school as well as special retreats. Adult education, either in Sunday Church School or separate from it, has also been included. Utilizing the conflict in the timely moments of a task group provides another possibility for education from conflict in the church. Intervention in a task process may be necessary in order that the task be continued creatively and constructively. Conflict can cause either conscious barriers or unconscious barriers to the successful and creative conclusion to the task. Brief, timely intervention may break those barriers and lead toward the desired end for all if constructive conflict education is introduced. Fear of the underlying conflict prohibits growth and progress for all.

In the very first chapter of this book, real illustrations were used to typify regular occurences which wait for constructive resolution in our churches today. One of them described the conflict of disruption of worship by the children of a regularly attending family. Older members in particular were unable to hear or concentrate in worship because of the distraction. The pastor desired whole families in worship yet realized the problems that children can create. The boycott of services by a number of the elderly made this conflict a crisis to be resolved. Can creative resolution and education be brought to such a situation?

Something creative did occur in the actual illustrative event. After the pastor attempted to talk to both the family and the elderly members who were objecting, he discovered that the real concern was about the raising of children. It was a general family concern as well as creating a by-product of concern among the elderly in the church. A meeting of those thus concerned about child raising was widened to include general community involvement. From this gathering came the idea to take advantage of a program already established called *Parent Effectiveness Training* by Thomas Gordon.[17]

The pastor and some of the church members sought out trained leadership and brought in this program, offering it to the whole community. A very positive experience for all came to both church and community stemming from the conflict in the worship service. Without the willingness to face the problem openly and constructively within the church, the positive value of families present in worship and the elderly's value of order and clarity for hearing could not be respected and preserved. The feeling of self-worth of the pastor and the respect for the worth of all parties to the conflict were points critical to the working out of this conflict. Gradually, the noise in worship lessened.

Self-trust and the worth of all persons form key structures upon which to build constructive conflict utilization. These psycho-theological based concepts should be grounded in the educational program of the church as well as throughout all functions and at all levels in the life of the church. If they are present, a foundation stone has been set to insure constructive experiences in the future when conflicts do arise within the congregation.

The purpose of this book is to give the rationale for a positive understanding of the dynamics of conflict in order to free persons to be creative in the midst of it for the benefit of all. That was the experience of the pastor and people in the prior example. May it be yours as well.

Notes

1. Robert L. Conrad, "Creative Learning in Christian Education: A Model of Creative Conflict" (Paper given at the APRRE meeting, St. Louis, Mo., Nov. 19, 1977).

2. Ibid., p. 17.

3. Ibid., p. 22.

4. "Week-End Pac for Late Teens," by Graded Press, Abingdon, 1969.

5. M. A. Lieberman, I. D. Yalom, and M. B. Miles, *Encounter Groups: First Facts* (New York: Basic Books, 1973), p. 415.

6. Ibid., p. 416.

7. Ibid., p. 417.

8. Ibid., p. 419.

9. Ibid.

10. Arthur L. Foster, "Exploring Conflict Dynamics through Non-Verbal Communication," *Chicago Theological Seminary Register* 59, no. 4 (May 1969): 32–39.

11. Virginia Satir, *Peoplemaking* (Palo Alto, Calif.: Science and Behavior Books, 1972), pp. 63–95.

12. "Win-As-Much-As-You-Can," in *A Handbook of Structured Experiences for Human Relations Training,* vol. 2, by J. W. Pfeiffer and J. E. Jones (Iowa City, Iowa: University Associates Press, 1970), pp. 66–69.

13. "Star Power," an educational simulation game developed by WBSI, La Jolla, Calif.: Simile II 1969.

14. "Powerplay," by George Peabody and Paul Dietterich (Naperville, Ill.: Powerplay, 1973).

15. R. W. Napier and M. K. Gershenfeld, *Instructor's Manual,* in *Groups: Theory and Experience* (Boston: Houghton Mifflin Co., 1973), pp. 4–8.

16. S. B. Simon, L. W. Howe, and H. Kirschenbaum, *Values Clarification* (New York: Hart Publishing Co., 1972).

17. Thomas Gordon, *Parent Effectiveness Training* (New York: P. H. Wyden, 1970).

Index of Names

277

Index of Subjects

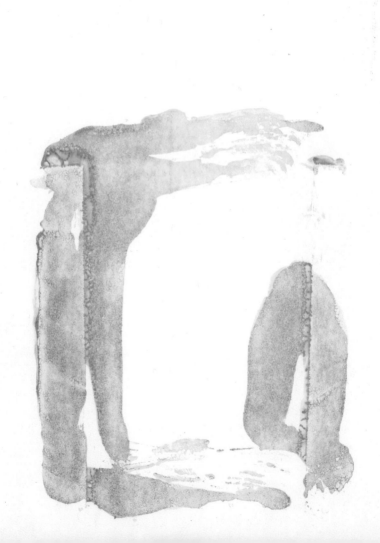